The Plan for the Child
Adoption or long-term fostering

Published by
British Association for Adoption and Fostering
(BAAF)
Skyline House
200 Union Street
London SE1 0LX
www.baaf.org.uk

Charity registration 275689

© Nigel Lowe and Mervyn Murch, 2002
   Reprinted 2003

**British Library Cataloguing in Publication
Data**
A catalogue record for this book is available from
the British Library

ISBN 1 903699 07 X

Project management by Shaila Shah, Director of
Publications, BAAF
Photograph on cover posed by models
by John Birdsall; www.JohnBirdsall.co.uk
Designed by Andrew Haig & Associates
Typeset by Avon DataSet Ltd, Bidford on Avon
Printed by Russell Press Ltd. (TU), Nottingham

The Plan for the Child
Adoption or long-term fostering

Nigel Lowe and Mervyn Murch,
Kay Bader, Margaret Borkowski,
Rosalie Copner, Cathy Lisles,
Jenny Shearman

Acknowledgements

This project was dependent on the goodwill, advice and assistance of many people. We wish to record our thanks to all those busy staff of the participant local authority social service departments who kindly agreed to be interviewed about their social work practice. Likewise our thanks to their other colleagues who often went to considerable lengths to facilitate our collection of data. We have taken care not to identify the authorities and to preserve the anonymity of their staff and that of all the case-related information which we have used.

The project was undertaken for, and funded by, the Department of Health and was linked to the Department's Quality Protects programme and with the Prime Minister's Review of Adoption which was undertaken concurrently by the Performance and Innovation Unit. The study was supported by a specially constituted Advisory Committee chaired by Julia Ridgway, Social Services Inspector. Other members of the committee were: Mike Brennan, Community Service Division, Department of Health; Felicity Collier, Chief Executive, BAAF; Janet Denny, Principal Planning and Policy Officer, Birmingham; Margaret Dight, Assistant Director, Catholic Children's Society; Val Hales, Service Manager, Leeds Social Services; Jennifer Jenkins, Grandparents Federation; Jeanne Kaniuk, Head of Adoption Service, Coram Family; Professor Roy Parker, Centre for Social Policy, Dartington; Professor David Quinton, School of Social Studies, University of Bristol; Professor Ian Sinclair, Social Work Research and Development Unit, University of York; and Professor John Triseliotis, Department of Social Work, University of Strathclyde. We are most grateful to them all for their expert advice in the planning and implementation of the research and for their helpful comments on earlier drafts of research papers. We also acknowledge advice from Professor Roger Bullock, Dartington Social Research Unit, during the planning phase of the project and the contribution of Dr Kerenza Hood to the project's statistical analysis.

The research itself was undertaken by a multidisciplinary team, several of whom had worked with the co-directors on previous adoption and family justice research projects. Nigel Lowe took the lead management role, supported by Mervyn Murch. Cathy Lisles was responsible for the design and management of statistical instruments. Kay Bader, Margaret Borkowski, Rosalie Copner and Jenny Shearman organised and undertook the fieldwork tasks – abstracting data from files and interviewing social work staff. Niki Bedford was the co-ordinating administrative secretary to the team. All the members have contributed to the compilation of the report.

Any errors and deficiencies in this report are the sole responsibility of the co-directors of the project and should not be attributed to any of our colleagues or advisers.

This work was undertaken by Cardiff University which received funding from the Department of Health. The views expressed in this publication are those of the authors and are not necessarily those of the Department of Health.

Nigel Lowe   **Mervyn Murch**
Professor of Law   Professor of Law
Cardiff Law School   Cardiff Law School

The Vernal Equinox, 2002

Contents

Part I

Introducing the Research

1 Introduction

1 Background to the research study

This publication concerns a relatively short investigation of the factors which determine the local authority decision to pursue adoption or long-term fostering for those looked after children for whom returning to their birth families is no longer thought possible. It follows on from several previous studies conducted by the Directors and their research teams (Murch and Lowe et al, 1993; Lowe et al, 1993; Lowe and Murch et al, 1999; Thomas and Beckford et al, 1999).

The study was undertaken at the request of the Department of Health at a time of unprecedented Government interest in the subject of adoption. It was conducted in the wake of the Government's "Quality Protects" initiative[1] designed to bring about improvements in child placement practice, the development of National Adoption Standards,[2] and the development by the Department of Health of *Framework for the Assessment of Children in Need and their Families* (Department of Health, 2000a).

This study was preceded by a broad-ranging programme of adoption policy related research (Parker, 1999) and was undertaken at a time when other investigations into the child placement fields were also being conducted (Broad et al, 2001; Hunt, 2001; Harwin and Owen, 2002).

Our investigations were also contemporaneous with ongoing preparation for adoption law reform which included publication of the Prime Minister's *Review of Adoption* (PIU, 2000) and the establishment of the Adoption Task Force. These developments have since led to the

---

[1] *Adoption – Achieving the right balance*, LAC (98) 20.

[2] See now *National Adoption Standards for England* (Department of Health, August 2001), for the implementation of which see LAC (2001) 33. These Standards were finalised following feedback on the consultation paper *Draft Practice Guidance to Support the National Adoption Standards of England* (Department of Health). It may be noted that at the time of writing Standards for Wales are still being considered.

introduction of the Adoption and Children Bill first in March 2001[3] and then in October 2001, which as we write, is currently before Parliament.

2 Aims

As agreed with the Department of Health in January 2000, this 15-month project aimed to examine the process which determines whether a child "looked after" by a local authority and who is in need of a "permanent family" is fostered or adopted.[4] In particular, the project investigated the possible reasons for the apparently wide variation in local authorities' use of adoption even between otherwise fairly similar agencies.

It also sought to examine the issue of delay both in the adoption and long-term fostering process investigating, in particular, what measures local authorities themselves have introduced since the initiation of the Quality Protects Programme to identify and combat the causes of delay. The term "delay" needs to be approached with caution. Although the Children Act 1989, s 1(2) sets out the general principle that delay in determining a question relating to the upbringing of a child is 'likely to prejudice the welfare of the child',[5] there are occasions when delay can be purposeful and positively beneficial. But in this study, in line with the intention of the Quality Protects Programme, we sought to focus upon detrimental delay.

In pursuing these aims it became apparent that it was not possible to look at the factors determining the long-term care of looked after children without also considering the wider context within which these decisions are made. Accordingly, the report explores a whole spectrum of issues to do with that process such as differences in local authority policy, record-keeping and social workers' knowledge, experience and understanding of child care issues.

All these issues interact and will influence the decision-making process in any individual case. Although ideally it would have been

---

[3] This original Bill fell when the General Election was called.
[4] For a discussion of the legal differences between adoption and fostering see below at para 3.1.
[5] The Adoption and Children Bill will introduce a similar principle to be applied in adoption proceedings.

useful to have explored and analysed their relative importance, given the time and resource constraints of this particular study, it was not possible to do more than provide a descriptive picture of the kinds of considerations to which those making or influencing these decisions paid attention. It will also be noted that in some places the findings occasionally seem contradictory and therefore merit further investigation and clarification.

As already intimated, the study was completed even before publication of the Adoption and Children Bill introduced in March 2001. However, in this publication we have added appropriate references to the second revised Bill. Furthermore, we refer to the *National Adoption Standards for England* rather than the draft version that we had to hand when undertaking the study.

3 Use of terms

3.1 The legal definition of adoption and fostering

Legally, there is a clear difference between adoption and fostering. It is only through adoption that a complete and irrevocable transfer of legal parentage can be effected – it being of the very essence of adoption that the prior *legal*[6] relationship between the adult(s) (usually the birth parents) and, consequently, the rest of the birth family, and the child is permanently extinguished and replaced by a new legal relationship between the adopters and the child. Moreover, adoption lasts for life: it does not end as other child-related orders do, when the child is 18.[7] Another point to bear in mind is that adoption can only be effected through a court order, so that there is a definite starting point to this important change in the child's status. In contrast, fostering does not change the child's status. Foster carers do not gain, and the birth parents do not lose, parental

---

[6] Adoption may not, however, sever the de facto links between the child and his or her birth family and indeed it is not unusual for older children to maintain some form of continuous contact with some members of the birth family (see Lowe and Murch *et al*, 1999, Ch 15).
[7] See the Adoption Act 1976 ss 12(1), (3) and 39. This basic status will not be altered by the Adoption and Children Bill.

THE PLAN FOR THE CHILD

responsibility. Instead, assuming, as will normally be the case in so-called long-term fostering, that the child is in local authority care, parental responsibility will be vested both in the local authority and the parents but with the former being in control. (The law has no specific cognizance of "long-term" fostering though those that have looked after a child for a period of time viz. one, three or five years are progressively better protected.)[8] Foster carers are effectively subject to continuing local authority scrutiny and control. Under the Foster Placement (Children) Regulations 1991,[9] local authorities are under a duty to supervise the placements (reg 6) and must not allow the placement to continue if it appears to them that the placement is no longer suitable (reg 7) and indeed foster carers are required to sign an agreement to allow the local authority to remove the child at their discretion (Sch 2, para 9). Although foster placements are, save in emergencies, required to be preceded by a written agreement (see Sch 3) there is nothing equivalent to an "adoption day" marking the making of an adoption order. Fostering will end when care ends. On the other hand, foster carers are entitled to such information about the child as is reasonable and can receive relatively generous (at

---

[8] Local authority foster carers with whom the child has his or her home for less than three years need to have the local authority's consent even to apply to the court for leave to seek a residence order, whereas those that have looked after the child for more than three years are *entitled* to apply (i.e. without the authority's consent or court leave) for a residence order (Children Act 1989, ss 9 (3), 10 (4)). Ironically, once foster carers have looked after a child for 12 months, they can apply to adopt him or her (Adoption Act 1976, s 13 (2)). [*Note:* this anomaly will be addressed by the Adoption and Children Bill inasmuch as local authority foster carers will be *entitled* to apply for a residence order once the child has had his or her home with them for one year rather than three years]. However, in this context, the law seeks to give stronger protection to those who have looked after the child for five years inasmuch that once notice of an interest to adopt has been made to the local authority, pursuant to s 22 of the 1976 Act, then *no-one* may remove the child from the applicants without court leave (s 28 of the 1976 Act). This protection, however, is not as advantageous as it might at first appear since, in any event, once notice of an intention to adopt has been given to the local authority they cannot then serve a s 30 notice for removal of the child from the applicants until the application has been disposed of (see s 31 of the 1976 Act). Furthermore, if, as will commonly be the case, the child is in local authority care, then the parent has no power to remove the child. A not dissimilar scheme is provided for by the Adoption and Children Bill.
[9] SI 1991/910.

any rate, compared with adoption allowances) foster allowances (see Sch 1).[10]

It ought also to be acknowledged at the outset that the Adoption and Children Bill will introduce a further important option of special guardianship but of course that option fell outside the scope of this study.[11]

3.2 Meaning of permanence

Whether it be by adoption or by long-term fostering, the aim should be, as the Department of Health's White Paper, *Adoption: A new approach* (Cm 5017, para 1.5) recognised, to provide children who are unable to live with their birth parents with a safe, stable and loving family. The key concept in our view is that of stability rather than the more commonly used term "permanence". The term "permanence" is in any event often used inconsistently. We note, for example, the inconsistent references in the Prime Minister's *Review of Adoption*[12] to the word "permanence": It is sometimes placed in juxtaposition to adoption, as in the recommendation to set out 'a clear national policy of permanence to be implemented by Local Authorities'; sometimes as a synonym for adoption, as in Recommendation 1 that 'the Government should set a target for increasing the use of adoption to provide successful permanent placements for children'; sometimes as a clear alternative, as in Recommendation 81 that 'the Government should consult on the details of a new legislative option for providing permanence short of adoption'. There is even a reference to 'real permanence' (para 4.2, p 51). Small wonder that there is confusion

---

[10] But see Chapter 3, para 4.5, below with regard to variations between short-term and long-term foster allowance rates. For the legality of differential rates cf *The Queen on the Application of L and Others v Manchester City Council; The Queen on the Application of R and Another v Manchester City Council* [2001] EWHC Admin 707, [2002] 1 FLR 43, discussed further in Chapter 3, p. 75. n 27. It is understood that adoption allowances are under review.

[11] But for further comment on the potential impact of special guardianship, see Chapter 6 at para 7.1.

[12] Similarly, the White Paper, supra, also refers to "permanence" in different ways. For example, at para 1.21 it is said that the Government 'will establish for children a full range of options for permanent families', whereas at para 2.12 it says 'only adoption provides legal permanence'.

in practice, for example, with Care Plans frequently stating grounds for so-called "permanence" rather than specifically for long-term fostering or adoption, which, as will be seen (see e.g. Chapter 3 at para 1), was evident among our sample authorities.

3.3 Other potentially confusing terms

In our initial interviews with social workers we discovered that some confusion existed about the terms "twin-tracking", "contingency planning" and "concurrent planning" (see further Chapter 5, para 2.3). Accordingly, in this report we use the following definitions:

Twin-tracking we define as a plan where the social worker is working with the birth parents on rehabilitation, while the child is in a foster placement and at the same time preparing the ground for a care order or a long-term or permanent placement elsewhere. This type of planning is sometimes known as parallel planning or dual track planning.[13]

Contingency planning occurs when a plan has been made and is being moved forward but at the same time a fall-back plan has been thought about and decided upon should the first plan fail. A contingency plan is a necessary requirement in court proceedings for a care or a freeing for adoption order.

Concurrent planning originates from a scheme pioneered in Seattle in the United States and is being piloted in Manchester,[14] Brighton and in the London Boroughs of Camden and Islington[15] with start-up funding

---

[13] Cf *The Draft Practice Guidance to Support the National Adoption Standards for England* (Department of Health) which describes what it refers to as "Parallel or Twin Track Planning", thus: 'The child remains with the birth parent/s or is placed with foster carers. A rehabilitation plan with timescales is in place. At the same time, the agency puts in place elements of a plan for an alternative permanent placement if the rehabilitation plan is unsuccessful.'

[14] This was the location of the first concurrent planning project in the UK and is known as the Goodman Report. See Katz L and Clatworthy B, *Innovation in Care Planning for Children* [1999] *Fam Law* 108 and *The Goodman Team–Concurrent Planning* [2001] *Fam Law* 301.

[15] In this regard the two London boroughs entered into service agreements with Coram Family, which is a charity set up by the Thomas Coram Foundation.

from the Department of Health. Concurrent planning was defined by Linda Katz, Programme Director of the Seattle Concurrent Planning Project as:

> ... *the process of working towards family reunification, while at the same time establishing an alternative permanent plan.*

As Butler-Sloss P has said:[16]

> *The policy is to pursue all the available options at once. Concurrent planning aims to provide children with one secure placement which would allow them to develop attachment to their carers while their birth family was assessed for rehabilitation.*

In other words, it involves the social worker working both with the child's foster carers as potential adopters, should rehabilitation fail, and with the birth parents to secure rehabilitation.

4 Outline method of approach

The study compared three local authorities (viz. one Metropolitan Borough, one Shire County and one London Borough) which, on the basis of statistical data available, appeared to make relatively high use of adoption with three comparable authorities (i.e. those with similar overall child care workloads) which made apparently low use of adoption. The investigation originally aimed to analyse in detail 40 case records in each selected authority, comprising 20 adoption and 20 fostering placements of children who had been "looked after" for a minimum of 12 months. This was to be followed by 40 interviews with selected case managers/ social workers involved in individual cases. However, for the reasons explained below (see post, paras 4.4 and 4.6), it was only possible to investigate 20 case records (comprising 10 adoption and 10 long-term

---

[16] In *M v London Borough of Islington and L* [2002] 1 FLR 95 at para [5]. Cf the Draft Practice Guidance which describes concurrent planning as a model which 'places the child with foster carers, who as well as providing temporary care for the child, act as a support to the birth parents in meeting the objectives of any rehabilitation plan. These carers have also been identified as available to be the child's adoptive parent if the rehabilitation plan should be successful.'

fostering placements) in each selected authority, and to conduct 26 interviews with case managers and social workers, though in addition each of the Directors of Social Services (or their assistants) were also interviewed.

4.1 Selection of local authorities

Using baseline data supplied by the Department of Health,[17] a sample of six authorities was chosen, from an overall total of 150 authorities, according to the following procedure:

The 46 Unitary Authorities were excluded as not being part of the original research brief. Nine additional authorities which did not exist prior to 1997–98 or had been affected by boundary changes were excluded on the basis that their trends in adoption would have also been affected (loss of adopters for example). A further 21 authorities outside this group which were already involved in the LAC (98) 20 data gathering exercise[18] were excluded so as to avoid adversely affecting their workload. Finally, 27 authorities, according to the Department's PAF Indicator[19] with an adoption rate of below 2.7 per cent (which were designated "low use") or above 5.6 per cent (which were designated "high use") as at 31 March 1998 were identified. Two authorities that were either particularly large or small, in terms of the numbers of children being looked after, were then excluded so that those selected could be roughly matched for workload.

A shortlist of 25 authorities was arrived at. Of the "low use" authorities on this list, 15 had less than 10 children adopted from local authority care during 1998–99. Nevertheless, it was hoped that it would still be possible to reach the required quota of 10 cases where the plan was for long-term fostering and 10 where the plan was for adoption at 31 March 1999.

---

[17] PAF Indicator C23 – Percentage of children looked after, adopted from local authority care 1998. But note this Indicator has been changed for 2001–2002, see Ch 6 at p. 140.

[18] LAC (98)20 *Adoption – Achieving the Right Balance*' was issued following comments from child care inspectors about the variable quality of adoption services. A survey of all social services departments was conducted in August 1999 to see how they were coping with the Circular.

[19] Ibid n 13.

Our rationale for deciding which of these 25 authorities should initially be approached to seek their agreement to participate in our research, was to obtain a sample of six authorities upon the basis of paired proximity: the pairing being on the basis of "high" and "low" use of adoption and the proximity so that the two Shires were in roughly the same region of the country, as were the two Metropolitan districts (the London authorities were, by definition, geographically proximate).

On this basis, 13 authorities (four Shires, four Metropolitan Boroughs and five London Boroughs) were initially chosen to be contacted though, for the reasons explained below, two further Shires were also subsequently approached.

4.2   Response from local authorities

Obtaining agreement in principle and establishing liaison to access information

Letters were sent in early March but response was slow. By mid-April, replies[20] had been received from the initial 13 authorities. Of these, two Metropolitan Boroughs, three London Boroughs but only one Shire authority agreed to participate.[21] To ensure that we had a requisite pair of Shire Counties, two further authorities were contacted. However, although one of these did agree to take part in the research, after further negotiation one of the "original" Shires responded positively, though not until the end of April, and it was that authority that was chosen. In this way we were able to select three appropriate pairs of authorities which, to preserve their anonymity, we have referred to throughout this report as London High and London Low, Metropolitan High and Metropolitan Low, Shire High and Shire Low.

Negotiating access proved time consuming and problematic. It proved difficult even to establish with whom the research team should liaise. Of

---

[20] In the case of one borough, however, agreement had to be re-negotiated as a record of the initial agreement had been mislaid by the authority.

[21] Among the reasons for authorities declining to take part in the study were that they were involved in internal care reviews, undergoing reorganisation of their children's services or were involved in other projects.

the final six authorities, only one Director replied immediately to our request to name a relevant liaison person with whom the team was to conduct all future negotiations. The remaining five took between two weeks and two-and-a-half months to do so. Permission to examine the files in London High was not finally negotiated until late August.

Obtaining case lists

Four of the authorities were able to produce lists of the cases meeting the research criteria (see below at para 4.5) to an agreed timescale, there being some delay in the remaining two as a result of the pressure of other work. However, our examination of these lists found that three of the authorities included cases which did not meet the research criteria.[22] In two of the authorities, the problem was quickly rectified, but in one, given the limited nature of the data produced, it was not possible to discover this error until after data collection was under way, resulting in some minor over-sampling.

4.3   Initial reconnaissance

An initial investigation of procedures and case files was carried out in two pilot local authorities not included in the main sample of six authorities. The purpose was threefold:

- to gain some knowledge about the structure, policies and procedures in specific types of authorities in relation to children's services, particularly in the areas of adoption and long-term fostering;
- to discover how varied the type and content of case records were likely to be;
- to estimate how long it would take to extract data from the case files.

After these pilot investigations, such was the degree of variation discovered that it was decided to carry out a similar reconnaissance in each of the six selected local authorities and even to allow for significant

---

[22] This was due to either misinterpretation of the selection criteria or mis-keying of the request into their computer software.

differences between individual area offices within each authority. In London High, however, a reconnaissance visit was abandoned because, as we previously explained, access was not finally given until the end of August. It was then decided that priority should be given to the collection of data in order to reduce delay in our research schedule.

4.4   The timetable

It was originally envisaged that, after the reconnaissance phase, the main fieldwork would be conducted from March to August 2000, with the analysis and writing up being undertaken between September and November. This timetable had to be revised at the end of April because it was taking so long to complete negotiations with some of the local authorities. More significantly, following the pilot reconnaissance, and given the delays already experienced, it became apparent that to keep to the timetable while maintaining a representative sample in each authority, the number of sample cases would have to be halved from 20 adoption and 20 long-term fostering cases to 10 of each.

In the event, the main fieldwork involving data collection from the files began in late May and, because of delays in gaining access to London High, was not finally completed until mid-September. This caused a knock-on effect to the social worker interview schedule, which was dependent on information from the case files, and likewise the Director interviews which could only be conducted when all the other fieldwork had been completed. The social worker and Director interviews were not completed until mid-November 2000 and early January 2001 respectively.

4.5   Case sample selection

Following discussion with members of the Advisory Committee, it was decided to focus upon children aged 12 years and under who had been looked after "for some time", as it was felt that these were the children most likely to be subject either to plans for long-term fostering or adoption, and to have possibly experienced delay. Thus, the criteria for selecting cases are defined as follows:

All children who were 12 and under on 31.3.99 (i.e. with a birth date no earlier than 1.4.86) and who have been looked after either contin-

uously between 1.4.98 and 31.3.99 or who have experienced three or more periods "in and out" of being looked after between 1.4.98 and 31.3.99 ("in and out" refers to distinct episodes of children being and ceasing to be "looked after" and not to mere changes in placement or legal status resulting in the start of a new care episode). This group may include children who have now ceased to be looked after.

The aims of the data collection exercise were:

- to provide a basic description of the cases meeting the research criteria in the six authorities;
- to facilitate the selection of cases for more detailed study where the plan was for long-term fostering or adoption;
- to discover the number of cases which did not have either of these plans;
- to assess whether the characteristics of the children who had a plan for long-term fostering differed from those who had a plan for adoption;
- to assess the nature of the decision-making process in relation to these two options;
- to quantify the extent of any "drift".

To achieve these aims, the sampling method (described in detail below) comprised a funnelling down mechanism in three stages. The first began with the recording of broad details of 807 cases from the six authorities meeting the research criteria (Stage 1). Stage 2 comprised a more detailed analysis of 220 cases systematically sampled from Stage 1. Stage 3 consisted of an in-depth examination of the files on 113 cases (59 long-term fostering and 54 adoption cases) sampled from Stage 2.[23]

It was sometimes not possible to determine from the case file when the period that the child became "looked after" began since respite care placements are not always counted on the Essential Information Record (EIR) as placement moves. Nevertheless, in practice the research team found that the case sample selection worked well.

---

[23] Although the local authority files in *all* these cases were examined, it should be noted that various documents, viz. the Essential Information Record and BAAF Form E, were sometimes incomplete or missing altogether from the file. See further Chapter 5, para 3.

The decision to include children with multiple admissions was based on the initially perceived view that it would help identify the extent of "drift". In retrospect, however, it was probably a hindrance to the project in that it reduced the usable numbers in the initial case selection sample for whom adoption or long-term foster care might have been appropriate and upon which the study concentrated.

Obtaining the Stage 1 cases

First, the authorities identified and produced lists of all the cases meeting the research criteria, resulting in a total of 807 cases, representing 37 per cent of all the children being looked after by these authorities on 31 March 1999. **Table 1** shows the actual percentage for each of the six authorities.

Table 1

Stage 1 cases meeting the research criteria in each of the six authorities as a percentage of all children being looked after by these authorities on 31 March 1999

Authority	Stage 1 selection as a % of all children looked after at 31 March 1999[24]
London High	33%
London Low	31%
Metro High	41%
Metro Low	46%
Shire High	47%
Shire Low	19%
Average	37%

[24] In order to abide by the undertaking given to participant local authorities that they would not be identified in publications resulting from this research, the actual numbers of cases given in the Department of Health figures upon which these percentages are based have been omitted.

The representativeness of the Stage 1 cases

The average number of children being looked after in local authorities in England on the 31 March 1999 was 369 (Department of Health, 2000c).[25] The average for our six local authorities was 366. The average number of cases meeting the research criteria produced by each of the local authorities was 135. However, individually, there were wide differences, from less than 70, to more than 220.[26]

As **Table 1** above shows, Shire Low produced the lowest percentage (19%) of their looked after population on 31 March 1999, whereas Shire High produced the highest percentage of 47 per cent. There may be many reasons for the wide variation in these percentages, such as differences in age distribution and working practices, all affecting the make-up of the looked after populations in these local authorities. For example, in Shire Low, the overall percentage of its looked after population aged under 10[27] on 31 March 1999 was among the lowest in England, at below 30 per cent.[28] Metro Low, on the other hand, had one of the highest percentages at above 50 per cent, the average for England as a whole being 44 per cent (Department of Health, 2000c).[29]

It is particularly notable that three of the local authorities had no children in the selected group who had been "in and out" of being looked after three or more times during the sample year period from 1 April 1998 to 31 March 1999. Metro High produced just one case, a boy of 11 who was subject to criminal proceedings, while the two shire authorities produced the highest number of this type of case. Shire Low produced only four such cases (6%) but, remarkably, Shire High produced 56 cases (31%). These mainly proved to be the result of the high use of respite care by that authority.

---

[25] Calculations based on Table A. Children in care/looked after at 31 March by age and sex, 1989–1999.

[26] Exact numbers are being withheld to avoid identifying the sample authorities.

[27] The age of 10 is referred to here so as to be able to compare with the nationally available "looked after" statistics which do not specifically refer to children aged up to 12 years.

[28] Again, precise figures are being avoided to preserve the anonymity of the sample authorities.

[29] See Table 8. Percentage of children aged under 10 years looked after by placement at 31 March 1997–99.

The local authorities were asked to provide some basic information about each of the cases; namely, age, gender, legal status and placement history. Surprisingly, given the number of studies that have stressed the importance of ethnicity, it was not possible to obtain any database information on that issue nor about religion and health because the local authority computer programmes did not permit the aggregation of such case-related data. In addition, information concerning the plan for the child at 31 March 1999 and at 31 March 2000 was requested but was also found not to be necessarily accessible from the computer systems.

Obtaining the Stage 2 sample

From the initial group of cases that met the research criteria, a systematic sample of either one in three or four was made, depending on the number of cases originally obtained from each local authority. Information was collected on a total of 220 cases, an average of 37 cases per local authority (27%). **Table 2** shows the percentage of cases sampled from the number of cases produced at Stage 1 of the data collection process for each local authority.

Table 2

Stage 2 cases sampled from those identified at Stage 1 for each of the six local authorities

Authority	Stage 2 sample as a % of Stage 1 cases
London High	32%
London Low	29%
Metro High	26%
Metro Low	25%
Shire High	25%
Shire Low	35%
Average	27%

A Data Collection System[30] was designed to record limited basic information on such items as age, gender, legal status, type of placement, reason for being looked after and the plan for the child at 31 March 1999 and

---

[30] See Appendix.

31 March 2000. In this way, data were collected on a cross section of the cases meeting the research criteria from each of the local authorities.

Representativeness of the Stage 2 sample

One initial difficulty in assessing the representativeness of the data collected was that there are few published national statistics which afford a direct comparison with the specific nature of the sample selected (i.e. children aged 12 years and under who had been looked after continuously for a year, or been looked after on three or more separate occasions during the preceding 12 months). However, the Department of Health provided us with a breakdown of information on children being continuously looked after as at 31 March 1999 by age and by different types of authority. Accordingly, comparisons could be made with cases in the research sample which met the criteria (that is, excluding for these purposes, those children in our sample who had been looked after on three or more occasions).[31]

Gender: The statistics provided by the Department of Health showed that on 31 March 1999, 54 per cent of the children who had been continuously looked after for a year or more were boys, and 46 per cent were girls. The figures for the Stage 2 sample were slightly different at 59 per cent and 41 per cent respectively. All of the authorities, bar Metro Low, had higher percentages of boys than the national statistics, and this was also reflected in comparison with the regional averages.

Age: The age distribution for the individual authorities was also different from the statistics provided by the Department of Health. Both of the Metropolitan authorities had more children in the younger age groups, and correspondingly fewer in the older age group. The Shire authorities and London High, however, followed the opposite pattern, with fewer younger children and more older. Indeed, 50 per cent of the continuously looked after children in the Stage 2 sample from Shire High were aged between 10 and 12 years. London Low was distinct in that there were

---

[31] For the profile of the whole sample, *including* those children in our sample who had been looked after on three or more occasions during the year, see Part II at Chapter 2 para 2.

Table 3
**Gender of continuously looked after children in the Stage 2 sample
compared with statistics from the Department of Health at 31 March 1999**

Authority / Region	Males	Females
London High	55%	45%
London Low	64%	36%
National London average	53%	47%
Metro High	59%	41%
Metro Low	53%	47%
National Metropolitan average	53%	47%
Shire High	60%	40%
Shire Low	70%	30%
National Shire average	54%	46%
Total	59%	41%
National average	54%	46%

fewer children than the national average in the five to nine age group, but more than the national average in the older and younger age groups. This pattern was very similar when comparison is made with the regional averages.

Legal status: Nationally, on 31 March 1999, 62 per cent of the children being looked after were subject to care orders, 34 per cent were being accommodated under s 20 of the Children Act 1989, and two per cent had been freed for adoption (Department of Health, 2000c).[32] In the research sample, the overall percentages for the children who were actually being looked after at that date were 77 per cent, 18 per cent and six per cent respectively.

[32] See Table C. *Children in care/looked after at 31 March by legal status, 1989–1999.* It should be noted that in our sample there were a greater proportion of children subject to care orders and proportionately fewer accommodated. This may be because our sample was limited to children who had been looked after for at least 12 months.

Table 4

Age of continuously looked after children in the Stage 2 Sample compared with statistics from the Department of Health as at 31 March 1999

Authority/Region	1–4	5–9	10–12
London High	23%	36%	42%
London Low	33%	30%	36%
National London Average	26%	38%	36%
Metro High	31%	44%	25%
Metro Low	29%	46%	26%
National Metropolitan Average	27%	42%	31%
Shire High	13%	37%	50%
Shire Low	26%	35%	39%
National Shire Average	24%	42%	34%
Total	27%	39%	35%
National Average	26%	41%	33%

Table 5

Legal status for all of the Stage 2 sample looked after on 31 March 1999

Legal	London High	London Low	Metro	Metro Low	Shire High	Shire	Total No: %
Care order	81%	82%	88%	89%	47%	62%	160 (77%)
Accommodated	19%	18%	9%	5%	36%	29%	37 (18%)
Freed for adoption	–	–	3%	5%	17%	10%	12 (6%)

Table 5 shows some marked differences between the Shire, Metropolitan and London authorities in relation to the percentage of children being looked after under a care order. In the selected London authorities it appears that no applications to "free a child for adoption" were made. Freeing was used to some extent in the Metropolitan authorities, but the percentage of care orders here was still high. In the Shire authorities, a greater proportion of the children were accommodated under s 20 of the Children Act 1989.

Obtaining the Stage 3 sample

The final part of the sampling process was to collect detailed information on the quota of 10 adoption and 10 long-term fostering cases for each local authority using a second Data Collection System.[33] In the end, it was not possible to obtain the full intended quota and the final sample comprised 113 rather than 120 cases, being one long-term fostering case short in London High, and six adoption cases short in Shire Low.[34]

The purpose of this stage of the research was altogether different, being aimed more at investigating the decision-making process with regard to the choice of plan, as found in the documents contained in the case files. Additionally, information was collected on: personal and family details (for example, significant adults and siblings), contact, the health details of the child, the birth family, special educational needs, placement history, reviews and previous attempts at rehabilitation with the child's family. The names of the last two social workers allocated to the case were recorded.

4.6   Social worker interviews

Social workers were interviewed to ascertain their views of the child care decision-making process. These interviews comprised questions both to illuminate the reasons for care plans where the records were unclear and to gather information about their understanding of policies relating to planning for children's long-term care.[35]

The original plan was to interview six social workers in each local authority. However, it became clear during the course of the fieldwork that there were at least two tiers of practitioner involved; namely, team managers (sometimes called "team leaders") and case workers. In four local authorities there was also an intermediary level of supervisory

---

[33] See Appendix.

[34] It was noted in the *Prime Minister's Review of Adoption*, op cit, at p 65, para 6.22, that in 1999 around 30 authorities placed fewer than three children for adoption, making adoption a "cottage industry" in those locations. In fact 115 out of 150 local authorities placed less than 20 children for adoption.

[35] For the outline interview schedule, see Appendix.

social worker. As team managers appeared to straddle the policy/practice divide and might therefore have a broader overview of the decision-making process within their team, it was considered appropriate to interview them in addition to the case workers. In this particular study we did not differentiate between those case workers who were employed specifically as "children's social workers" and those who were "family placement social workers". Consequently we do not comment on the way that their roles interact (see Lowe and Murch *et al*, 1999, pp. 401–03 & 411).

Due to a reduced sample of core cases, coupled with timetabling constraints, it was decided to attempt to conduct interviews with two team managers and two case workers in each local authority. Individuals were selected from different teams in order to cover the possibility that policies might differ between the teams, and on the basis of their involvement in the greatest number of cases. A total of 26 interviews were conducted.

4.7   Interviews with Directors

To help to "balance" the study it was decided to interview the six Directors of Social Services in order to obtain their views about adoption and long-term fostering policies in their authorities. These interviews were conducted between November 2000 and January 2001. Three were with Directors and three were with Assistant Directors with special responsibility for children's services. For convenience, however, we will refer to all six as "Directors" throughout the following report.

Our aim was to ascertain their views of the policy context within which their particular authority decided whether a looked after child was fostered or adopted. In this respect what they told us supplemented and helped to balance the main quantitative findings gleaned from our survey of case files and the more qualitative information from the interviews with the 26 social workers.

The interviews were based upon a checklist of questions designed to elicit the Directors' views as to how their department established child care priorities and had responded to the Government's Quality Protects initiative. The interviews were fairly informal and sufficiently open so that Directors could direct our attention to their particular child care concerns.[36] In this way, although obviously individual Directors had their own particular worries, we hoped to identify some key general themes in their overall perspective which would help us obtain a broad background picture against which to place our more specific findings.

At least four of the Directors had extensive child care experience – in two instances more than 20 years. They had seen, therefore, many practice and policy changes and were able to evaluate their impact on such matters as training, recruitment and the current state of staff morale.

References

Broad B, Hayes R and Rushforth C (2001), *Kith and Kin: Kinship care for vulnerable young people*, London: National Children's Bureau

Clatworthy B (2001), 'The Goodman team – concurrent planning', *Family Law Quarterly*, 301

Department of Health (2001), *National Adoption Standards for England*, London: Department of Health

Department of Health (2000a), *Assessing Children in Need and their Families: Practice guidance*, London: Department of Health

Department of Health (2000b), *Adoption: A new approach*, London: Department of Health

Department of Health (2000c), *Children Looked After by Local Authorities – Year ending 31 March 1999*, London: Department of Health

Harwin J and Owen M (2002), 'A study of care plans and their implementation and their relevance for Re W & B and Re W [care plan]', in Thorpe J and Cowton C (eds), *Delight and Dole: The Children Act 10 years on*, Jordans Publishing Ltd

Hunt J (2001), 'Kinship care, child protection and the courts', in Broad B (ed), *Kinship Care: The placement choice for children and young people*, Lyme Regis: Russell House Publishing

Katz L and Clatworthy B (1999), 'Innovation in care planning for children', *Family Law Quarterly*, 108

---

[36] For the outline interview schedule, see Appendix.

Lowe N with Borkowski M, Copner R, Griew K and Murch M (1993), *Report of the Research into the Use and Practice of the Freeing for Adoption Provisions*, London: HMSO

Lowe N and Murch M, Borkowski M, Weaver A, Beckford V with Thomas C (1999), *Supporting Adoption – Reframing the approach*, London: BAAF

Murch M, Lowe N, Borkowski M, Copner R and Griew K (1993), *Pathways to Adoption: Research Project*, London: HMSO

Parker R (ed) (1999), *Adoption Now: Messages from research*, London: Department of Health

Performance and Innovation Unit (PIU) (2000), *Prime Minister's Review of Adoption*, London: Cabinet Office

Thomas C and Beckford V with Lowe N and Murch M (1999), *Adopted Children Speaking*, London: BAAF

Part II

Findings

2 The profile of the sample children

1 Introduction

To put our findings in context, we present an analysis of the basic profile of the 220 children in the Stage 2 sample.

2 The characteristics of the children[1]

2.1 Gender

The Stage 2 sample comprised 59 per cent boys and 41 per cent girls overall, but while boys always constituted the majority, as **Table 6** below shows, there were variations between authorities with Shire Low having the largest proportion of boys (67%) and Metro Low having the smallest (53%).

Table 6
Gender by local authority[2]

Authority	Male	Female
London High	55%	45%
London Low	64%	36%
Metro High	61%	39%
Metro Low	53%	47%
Shire High	59%	41%
Shire Low	67%	33%
TOTAL	59%	41%

---

[1] Note that the following analysis is of the *whole* Stage 2 sample. Compare the discussion in Chapter 1, p. 18 which only concerns those in the sample who had been continuously looked after for 12 months and therefore excluded those who had been looked after on three or more occasions during the year.

[2] The percentages included in these tables will not always total 100 as a result of rounding.

2.2   Age

Age at 31 March 1999

The research criteria restricted the age group of the sample to children aged 12 and under on 31 March 1999, who had been looked after continuously from 1 April 1998 until 31 March 1999 or who had been "in and out" of being looked after at least three times during that period. Thus, the sample did not contain children aged under one year or 13 and above, on 31 March 1999.

The mean age for the children in our sample at 31 March 1999 was 7.8 years. **Table 7** opposite shows that one-third of the children were between one and four years of age at 31 March 1999, with the greatest number being between five and nine. Just under one-quarter were aged 10 and over.

There were variations between the authorities with London High having the fewest children in the 1–4 age category (23%) and Metro Low the fewest in the 10 and over group (9%). At the other extreme, Metro Low had the most in the 1–4 category (42%) and Shire Low in the 10 and over (33%). Children within the 5–9 age range varied from 52 per cent in Metro High to 38 per cent in Shire Low. The age distributions of the children in the two shire counties are the most similar of the pairs of authorities, whereas the metropolitan areas show the most marked differences, particularly in respect to the older children. Since, as will be seen,[3] the child's age is an important factor in deciding whether to place for adoption or long-term fostering, these different age profiles are significant.

Age at start of latest episode of being looked after

With regard to the children who were looked after continuously between 1 April 1998 and 31 March 1999 (204 cases), it was possible to identify their age at the start of their last episode of being looked after. Seven children started to be looked after from the day that they were born, with 14 starting to be looked after within a month of their birth. The age at which the oldest child started to be looked after was 11.

---

[3] See Chapter 3, para 2.1.

Table 7
Age profile at 31 March 1999 by local authority

Authority	1–4	5–9	10 & over
London High	23%	45%	32%
London Low	36%	39%	24%
Metro High	30%	52%	18%
Metro Low	42%	49%	9%
Shire High	30%	39%	32%
Shire Low	29%	38%	33%
TOTAL	33%	44%	23%

Table 8 below shows that there were large differences between both the mean and median age at the start of the last episode of being looked after for these children according to their local authority.

Table 8
Mean and median age at start of latest episode of being looked after by local authority

Authority	London High	London Low	Metro High	Metro Low	Shire High	Shire Low	TOTAL N = 204
Mean	4.7	3.8	3.8	4.0	5.8	3.7	4.3
Median	5.4	2.8	3.6	3.3	5.4	3.3	3.9

The difference in these figures is best illustrated through the use of the box plots (see Figures 1 and 2 below). It can be seen that the distributions for the "High" users of adoption were broader than those of the "Low" users, and that while the medians for the Metropolitan authorities were quite close together, those for the other pairs of authorities (particularly the Shires) were dissimilar.

Paradoxically, what the profile seems to show is that in the authorities in which the adoption rate was said to be high, the children were older at the start of the latest episode of being looked after, than in those authorities which were considered to have a low rate of adoption. However, a different picture emerged when examining the age at which the children last started

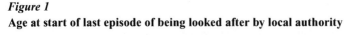

Figure 1
Age at start of last episode of being looked after by local authority

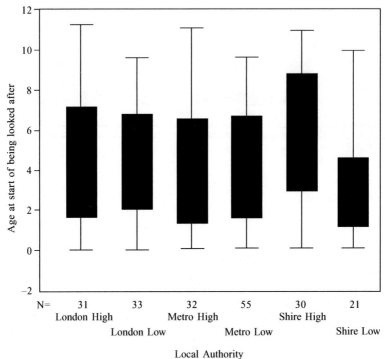

to be looked after according to the plan for the child at 31 March 1999. The mean age at starting to be looked after for children with plans for long-term fostering was 5.4 years, while for those with plans for adoption it was much lower at 2.7 years.[4] The distribution of these ages is shown in **Figure 2** opposite and clearly reveals that the overall age profile of

---

[4] Note: in two cases there was said to be a plan both for adoption and long-term fostering. The mean age for these was 1.1 years. The mean age for children with "other plans" was 4.6 years. "Other plans" refers to cases where the plan was neither adoption nor long-term fostering; namely, where the child was to remain with or to be returned to the birth family or was living with relatives other than as a foster child or was subject to a special residential placement.

Figure 2[5]

Age at start of last episode of being looked after by plan for the child at 31 March 1999

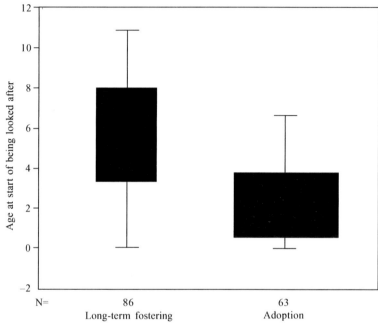

children for whom the plan was adoption was significantly lower than for those for whom the plan was long-term fostering.

2.3 Ethnicity, cultural identity, language and religion

Except for the London authorities, data on the ethnicity of the children's parents were incomplete with information missing in 16 per cent of the case files (N = 35) in relation to mothers and 21 per cent (N = 46) in relation to fathers. Similarly, information about the child's cultural identity

---

[5] Not including two cases in which there was said to be a plan both for adoption and long-term fostering.

was also missing in 19 per cent of the cases (N = 42).[6] This notable absence of data is worrying.

So far as mothers were concerned, 73 per cent were said to be white, five per cent black (including 2% black Caribbean and 1% black African), three per cent of mixed heritage and three per cent Asian.[7] So far as birth fathers were concerned, the respective proportions were 65 per cent white (slightly lower than mothers), eight per cent black (including 4% black Caribbean and 3% black African), five per cent Asian and two per cent of mixed heritage.[8]

Table 9 below shows the ethnic origin of the birth mother and father by the local authority (missing cases are not included).

Table 9
Ethnic origin of birth mother and father by local authority

Ethnic origin	London High	London Low	Metro High	Metro Low	Shire High	Shire Low	TOTAL No: %
Birth mother:							
White	77%	64%	91%	98%	97%	93%	161 (87%)
Black, Mixed, Asian	23%	36%	9%	2%	3%	7%	24 (13%)
Birth father:							
White	71%	58%	84%	91%	100%	87%	142 (82%)
Black, Mixed, Asian	29%	42%	16%	9%	–	13%	32 (18%)

Table 9 also shows that only a small percentage of birth mothers of minority ethnic origin were to be found outside London. This was also true in relation to the birth father, although the proportion was slightly greater in Metro High.

---

[6] While there were missing data in all the authorities, it was most noticeably absent in Shire Low (42%, N = 10 missing) and Shire High (30%, N=13 missing).

[7] If missing data are excluded, the respective proportions were 87% white, 6% black (including 3% black Caribbean and 3% African), 4% of mixed heritage and 3% Asian.

[8] If missing data are excluded, the respective proportions were 82% white, 10% black (comprising 5% black Caribbean and 5% black African), 5% Asian and 2% of mixed heritage.

In relation to the child's cultural identity, 70 per cent of the case files[9] gave this as white, with three per cent mixed, three per cent black, two per cent each black British and British Asian, and one per cent Asian.[10] As one would expect, this distribution of children's cultural identity by authority followed the same pattern as for the ethnic origin of the parents, with a wider range of cultural identities being found in the London authorities.

In over three-quarters of the case files,[11] the first language was given as English (78 per cent), with eight children having other languages as their first language (4%) including Farsi, Lingala, Punjabi and Portuguese. Three children had no speech or understanding at all (1%). Only 44 per cent (N = 96) of the case files indicated that the child had a religion and only 25 of these children (26%) were said to be practising that religion.

2.4 Ongoing health conditions/disabilities

Based on information recorded in the Essential Information Record, in 38 per cent of the case files the child was said to have an ongoing health condition or disability (N = 83).[12] Boys were over-represented in this group, with nearly two-thirds of the children being male (65%, N = 54).

The most frequently reported problems were: general learning disabilities (16 cases); asthma (16 cases); eczema (15 cases); hearing impairment (9 cases); speech difficulties (8 cases) and visual impairment (6 cases). Other conditions such as HIV infection (5 cases); sickle cell anaemia (2 cases); cerebral palsy (2 cases); cancer (1 case); Down's Syndrome (1 case); and bowel and bladder disorders (4 cases). Severe global development delay (3 cases) and severe disabilities (3 cases) were also mentioned. The research team was not in a position to judge how severe these conditions may have been.

---

[9] Note: 19% of files did not have this information.

[10] The coding information on ethnicity and cultural identity follows that used by the LAC (98) 20 research project *Adoption Planning for Children*.

[11] Note: these data were missing in relation to 17% of the children (N = 37).

[12] Note: individual children could have more than one condition. In addition, it might be noted that, according to the Department of Health's White Paper *Adoption: A new approach* (2000a) Cm 5017, at para 2.4, 67% of all looked after children have an identifiable mental health problem and an estimated 30% have statements of educational need.

2.5 Legal status

As at 31 March 1999

Table 10 below shows that, as at 31 March 1999, 73 per cent of these looked after children were subject to care orders.[13] Eleven children in the Shire authorities were not actually being looked after on that date. These included nine children who were at home on that date having previously experienced short periods of respite care.[14]

Table 10 also shows that there was a marked variation between the authorities, with notably lower proportions of children subject to care orders in the Shires but with correspondingly higher proportions of children both accommodated and freed for adoption. Neither of the London Boroughs sampled included any children freed for adoption.[15] It is interesting to note that freeing for adoption was not used in respect of any child aged 10 and over.

Table 10
Legal status at 31 March 1999 by local authority

Legal status	London High	London Low	Metro High	Metro Low	Shire High	Shire Low	TOTAL No: %
Care orders	81%	82%	88%	89%	39%	54%	160 (73%)
Accommodated under s 20 Children Act 1989	19%	18%	9%	5%	30%	25%	37 (17%)
Freed for adoption	–	–	3%	5%	14%	8%	12 (5%)
Not looked after on that date	–	–	–	–	18%	13%	11 (5%)

---

[13] Which, for these purposes, includes interim care orders, deemed care orders (i.e. former wards of court who are deemed to be in care pursuant to the Children Act 1989, Sch 14 para 15(2)) and supervision orders with a residence requirement made under either the Children and Young Persons Act 1969, s 12AA or the Children Act 1989, Sch 14, para 36(4)(d).

[14] As a matter of law it might be noted that, if children are placed with foster carers, they are classified as accommodated at home while being "looked after". Similarly, children placed in respite care for more than 24 hours are also "looked after": Children Act 1989, s 22(2).

[15] For a discussion of the use of freeing for adoption proceedings, see Chapter 5, p. 116.

Not all the children whose case files were examined had been looked after continuously from 1 April 1998 until 31 March 1999. Sixteen children (7%) had been "in and out" three or more times during the year. As stated above, the majority of these children were receiving respite care from the local authority, although there was one child in Metro High under a supervision order with a residence requirement.

As at 31 March 2000

Of the 220 case files examined, 34 children (16%) had ceased to be looked after by 31 March 2000.[16] Of the remaining 186 children, the majority (79%) were subject to care orders, with 16 per cent accommodated and five per cent freed for adoption. This overall profile reflects that of a year earlier.

2.6   Reason for being looked after

The most frequently stated reason in the file for the children being looked after on 31 March 1999, was that the child was at risk of being abused or neglected (N = 132, 63%). This was particularly the case for the Metropolitan authorities and London Low. Other reasons given included parents needing relief (17 cases = 8%), parents' ill-health (9 cases = 4%) and continuing preventive work with the family while the child was being looked after (9 cases = 4%).[17] Only three children (1%), were being looked after at the request of their parents as a preliminary to adoption. It should be cautioned, however, that in 11 per cent of the cases examined (N = 22 children) the reason for being looked after could not be found in the file. Metro Low and Shire Low did not have this information in a third of the case files examined.

---

[16] See further below at para 3.3.

[17] These reasons reflect the national statistics inasmuch as the top three reasons for being looked after are abuse/neglect, parental relief, parental ill-health (see Table E in Department of Health, 2000b).

3 The plan for the child

3.1 As at 31 March 1999

For ease of comparison, the data collected on the plan for the child have been analysed under three major types, namely, adoption, long-term fostering, and "other" (which for this purpose essentially means where the *plan* for the child is something other than long-term fostering or adoption).[18] It should be noted, however, that in two cases (one each in London High and Shire High) the plan was said to be both for adoption and long-term fostering (these are not included in Table 11 below).

Table 11
Plan for the child at 31 March 1999 by local authority

Plan	London High	London Low	Metro High	Metro Low	Shire High	Shire Low	TOTAL[19] No: %
Long-term fostering	29%	30%	39%	47%	41%	46%	87 (40%)
Adoption	45%	42%	30%	24%	21%	17%	64 (29%)
Other	23%	27%	30%	29%	36%	38%	67 (31%)

Table 11 above shows that, at 31 March 1999, long-term fostering was the plan for 40 per cent of the children overall. This included 16 cases (7% of the sample) where the plan was for long-term fostering with relatives.[20] Adoption was the plan for 29 per cent of the children.[21] Of the

---

[18] See further note 4 above.

[19] Additionally, 11 children who were not being looked after on 31 March 1999 have been added into the groups which correspond to those which they would have been part of *on the commencement of their very next episode of being looked after*. Thus, 10 of the children have been added into the "other" category and one to the adoption group. This procedure was not found to have any effect on the relative order of the six authorities in relation to their use of different plans.

[20] Nine of these cases were in Metro Low, revealing it to be a particularly strong user of relatives in long-term planning, which in terms of performance indicators might well be considered more positive than adoption.

[21] Although, as already noted, in two cases the plan was expressed to be both for long-term fostering and adoption.

remaining 31 per cent, the majority of the plans for the child were to remain with the birth family through the provision of support services, which accounted for half of this group (32 cases), or to return home (16 cases) in either the short or longer term to the birth parents or, in one case, to the birth father and a stepmother. Excluding these "other" plans, 58 per cent of the children were subject to a plan for long-term fostering as against 42 per cent for adoption.

The majority of children for whom the plan was long-term fostering were subject to care orders (70 cases = 80%). This was also true for adoption (46 cases = 72%) and for "other" plans (42 cases = 63%).

Plans for adoption were noticeably more common in relation to children aged one to four years. Sixty-four per cent of the children with a plan for adoption were in this age category, compared with only 25 per cent in the 5–9 age group and only 11 per cent for those aged 10 or more. The mean age at 31 March 1999 for children with plans for adoption was 5.5 years whereas for those for whom the plan was long-term fostering the mean age was 9.6 years. The mean age of children with "other" plans was 7.8 years.

It might have been expected that, based on the national statistics, the three authorities selected as making a high use of adoption would have had the highest percentage of cases where adoption was the plan. Remarkably, this was not always so. Rather, the pattern seems to be based more upon the type of authority. For example, *both* London authorities made higher than average use of adoption plans, whereas both the Shire authorities were noticeably lower than average (with London Low having twice the percentage of Shire High). Nevertheless, when comparison is made by type of authority, the so-called "high use" authorities have a higher incidence of planning for adoption than their "low use" counterparts.

3.2 As at 31 March 2000

Of the 220 case files which were examined, 34 of the children (16%) were not being looked after by the local authorities on 31 March 2000. Eight of these children had been receiving periodic respite care from the local authorities, and were not looked after on that date; the remaining 26 (12%) had ceased to be looked after. These included 16 children who had been adopted, five who were returned to their birth family and four in respect of whom the care order had been discharged.

Table 12 below shows the plan for the child at 31 March 2000, for the 194 children who were still being looked after by the local authority in any capacity.[22]

Table 12
Plan for the child at 31 March 2000 by local authority

Plan	London High[23]	London Low	Metro High	Metro Low	Shire High[24]	Shire Low	TOTAL[25] No: %
Long-term fostering	32%	39%	50%	59%	46%	48%	91 (47%)
Adoption	36%	36%	23%	19%	12%	13%	44 (23%)
Other	29%	26%	27%	23%	39%	39%	57 (29%)

By 31 March 2000, the number of plans for long-term fostering had risen in each authority,[26] although this was less marked in three of the authorities (London High, Shire High and Shire Low) while those for adoption had fallen, partly as a result of 16 children who had been adopted during the previous year and eight who were no longer being looked after, but also as a result of changes in plan, a subject which is discussed further below.[27]

Looking at the overall pattern of the plans, it will be noted that the London authorities still had the highest proportion of adoption plans and the lowest of long-term fostering plans. The Metropolitan authorities continued to maintain the middle ground for adoption plans but with the

---

[22] This includes eight children who had been in respite care but who were not being looked after on the relevant date.

[23] In addition, there was one case (4%) in which there was said to be a plan both for long-term fostering and adoption.

[24] In addition, there was one case (3%) in which there was said to be a plan both for long-term fostering and adoption.

[25] In addition, there were two cases (1%) in which there was said to be a plan both for long-term fostering and adoption.

[26] Excluding "other" plans, 67% of the children were subject to a plan for long-term fostering as against 33% for adoption.

[27] See para 3.3 below.

highest proportion of long-term fostering plans. The Shire authorities (understandably in the case of Shire High given their large number of adoptions in the previous year) had the lowest proportion of adoption plans but the highest of "other" plans. What these findings illustrate is how misleading a single snapshot analysis of the looked after children population in a local authority can be.

3.3 Changes of plan

Of the 186 children who were still being looked after on 31 March 2000,[28] a striking 35 (19 per cent) had experienced a change of plan during the preceding year. In six cases there was a move from a plan for long-term fostering to firm plans for rehabilitation or discharge of the care order, while in two further cases, foster carers wished to adopt the child or were seeking a residence order. The plans for 10 of the remaining 26 children[29] had been for rehabilitation, but had been changed to long-term fostering or adoption. For a further five children, the change of plan related to moves into residential accommodation, as this was now seen as best meeting the needs of the child.

In five cases, the plan had changed from adoption or adoption and long-term fostering to long-term fostering, or from adoption to adoption and long-term fostering. One of these changes (in London Low) was the result of the current carers of the child no longer wishing to adopt, but being prepared to foster the child, and three because of the delay that was being experienced in identifying suitable adopters (two in London High, one in Metro Low).[30] In the final case, in London Low, there was no explanation for this change of plan on the file, although a new social worker had just taken over the case.

---

[28] I.e. excluding eight children who were subject to respite care at various times during the research project.

[29] Information on the reasons for one change of plan was not on the file.

[30] For example, as one social worker from Metro Low said when interviewed: 'There was extensive advertising across the country for the child and two siblings, but no adopters were found. As a result, the long-term plans were reviewed in August 1999 and the decision was made for the child to stay with their current carers with a view to the placement becoming long-term.'

There were six cases in which disruption to a placement had caused a change in plan, four in relation to plans for long-term fostering (in London High, London Low, Shire High and Metro Low) and two with regard to plans for adoption (in London High and Metro Low). All these plans were being reassessed. We found one case (in Shire Low) in which, following the disruption of a long-term placement, the plan remained for long-term fostering.

3.4 Current placement (at 31 March 2000)

Table 13
Placement at 31 March 2000 by local authority[31]

Placement	London High	London Low	Metro High	Metro Low	Shire High	Shire Low	TOTAL No: %
Foster placement	44%	63%	58%	68%	68%	78%	115 (63%)
Placed for adoption	26%	17%	19%	13%	13%	11%	30 (17%)
Placed with a parent/ relative under a care order	7%	13%	23%	11%	7%	6%	21 (12%)
Residential home or school	22%	7%	0%	8%	11%	6%	16 (9%)

Nearly two-thirds of our sample of looked after children were in a foster placement (N = 115). Of these, 62 per cent were in a foster placement *within* the local authority (N = 71), and 17 per cent were in a foster placement with a relative or friend either inside or outside the local authority (N = 20). Interestingly, 13 of the children who were in a foster placement with a relative or friend were to be found in Metro Low (65%).[32]

Less than a fifth (17%) of the children were placed for adoption. Of these, 57 per cent (N = 17) were aged between one and four years of age, with only one-third (N = 10) aged between five and nine, and 10 per cent aged 10 and over (N = 3).

---

[31] Data were unavailable on four cases.

[32] Furthermore, two of the three children in our sample to be adopted by relatives were also in Metro Low.

Relatively few children were placed with a parent or other relative under a care order or in a residential home or school. However, Metro High and London High showed the highest use of these two placement types respectively. There were three times as many boys as girls placed in residential homes and schools, all of whom were five years of age or older.

4 Summary

4.1 Basic profile of the Stage 2 sample of children

Two-hundred-and-twenty children aged between one and 13 years had either been continuously looked after for 12 months ending 31 March 1999 or had been "in and out" of being looked after at least three times during that period. The children's profile broke down as follows:

- 59% boys; 41% girls;
- 33% aged 1–4 years; 44% aged 5–9 years; 23% aged 10–12 years;
- The mean age of children at start of last episode of being looked after was 5.4 years for those for whom the plan was long-term fostering, but only 2.7 years for those for whom adoption was the plan;
- 82% were white; 10% black; 5% Asian and 2% mixed heritage;
- 38% had ongoing health conditions or disabilities but this was more pronounced for boys (41% of boys as opposed to 21% of girls);
- 73% of children were subject to care orders; 17% accommodated; 5% freed for adoption (5% not looked after on 31 March 1999);
- The most common reasons for being looked after were: 63% risk of abuse or neglect; 8% parents needed relief; 4% parents' ill-health; 4% to enable continuing preventive work with the family; 11% there was no reason stated.

4.2 The plan for the child as at 31 March 1999

Overall the proportion of the plans broke down as follows:

- 40% long-term fostering (including 7% by relatives); 29% adoption and 31% neither long-term fostering nor adoption ("other plans");
- Excluding "other" plans, 58% of children were subject to a plan for long-term fostering and 42% for adoption;

BUT

- There were large variations between authorities ranging from 73% long-term fostering/27% adoption in Shire Low to 39% long-term fostering/61% adoption in London High.
- **Note**: on these calculations London Low had a higher proportion of adoption plans than either Metro High or Shire High;
- 80% of children, where long-term fostering was the plan, were subject to care orders, as opposed to 72% for whom adoption was the plan;
- The mean age of children for whom long-term fostering was the plan was 9.6 years as opposed to 5.5 years for whom adoption was the plan;
- Of the children for whom adoption was the plan, 64% were aged 1–4 years, 25% 5–9 years and 11% 10–12 years.

4.3   The plan for the child as at 31 March 2000

- 47% long-term fostering; 23% adoption (but only 17% placed for adoption), 29% "other";
  BUT
- During the previous 12 months, 16 (7%) children were adopted; five (2%) were returned to birth family and for four (2%) in respect of whom the care order had been discharged;
- 35 children (19%) had experienced a change of plan;
- For six children (3%) the change of plan was caused by a disruption of the placement – in four cases, long-term fostering and in two, adoption.

4.4   The child's placement as at 31 March 2000

- 63% of children were in a foster placement;
- 17% were placed for adoption;
- 12% were placed with a parent or relative under a care order; and
- 9% were placed in a residential home or school.

References

Department of Health (2000a), *Adoption: A new approach*, London: Department of Health

Department of Health (2000b), *Children Looked After by Local Authorities – Year ending 31 March 1999*, London: Department of Health

3 Factors affecting long-term planning

1 Introduction

In this chapter we discuss our findings concerning the factors that affect decision-making and those which influence the execution of the plan for the long-term care of children being looked after by local authorities. In doing so we draw first on the data obtained from the 113 case files obtained in Stage 3.[1] These provided profiles and characteristics of the children which we were able to analyse and compare in relation to the care plans for those children. Secondly, we use data from the factors recorded in the children's case files given as reasons for deciding upon their long-term plans. Thirdly, we rely upon the responses of the social workers whom we interviewed when asked what factors they took into account in formulating long-term plans for specific children in the Stage 3 sample for whom they were responsible. We also report on the general views of the 26 social workers interviewed about what factors they would take into account when making plans for adoption or long-term fostering and on the views of the Directors of Social Services concerning more generalised reasoning and policy concerning long-term planning for children.

So far as the Stage 3 data are concerned, the analysis of the factors affecting the long-term plan for the children in the sample was done on the basis of the plan for the child as at 31 March 1999. Some of the children would have experienced a change of plan in the ensuing year.

Eighty-seven of the 113[2] case files examined had reasons for the plan for the child recorded in either the Care Plan or the Statutory Review document. Of these 87 cases, the research team was able to identify those which had "clear" reasons for the option chosen and those which had

---

[1] See Chapter 1, p21.

[2] As previously stated, it was not possible to obtain the full intended quota of 10 adoption and 10 long-term fostering cases in each of the six local authorities and the final sample comprised 113 rather than 120 cases, 59 long-term fostering cases and 54 adoption cases.

only "general" reasons recorded. A "clear" reason was defined as one which specifically related to the plan for adoption or long-term fostering. A "general" reason was defined as one that did not specifically relate to the long-term plan being formulated. "General" reasons included "rehabilitation not possible" and "no suitable relatives" which, in our view, explained why the child could not return home and would therefore be in need of a long-term alternative care arrangement, but did not provide reasoning as to the form of that care arrangement. Only 69 cases (comprising 29 adoption and 40 long-term fostering) which had clear reasons on file for the Care Plan were included in the analysis of the factors affecting decision-making.

Twenty-six social workers were interviewed about 40 cases. However, two were not able to comment on the specific decision-making process since they had not been responsible for the case at the time the plan was made. In a further two cases only general reasons were given. This therefore provided 36 cases (17 adoption and 19 long-term fostering) where clear reasons for the plan were provided by social workers in the interviews.[3] Wherever possible we inter-relate the different sources of data. However, in some areas, for example what we have termed "organisational-related factors", our sole source of information is from our interviews. In this respect we should perhaps be cautious in accepting all that is said, for while such evidence testifies to the practitioners' own beliefs about, for example, the factors that might affect their approaches – individually or collectively within the agency – to child care planning, it is also likely to contain a degree of rationalisation if not optimism.

We have organised our material to reflect what we have identified as the three major types of factors affecting both the planning and the execution of the plan, namely, those relating to the child, those that we describe as "family-related" and those we term "organisational-related".

In the ensuing discussion it is worth bearing in mind that there is an important distinction between the planning and its execution: what is ideal has inevitably to be tempered by what is possible. As a social worker in London High put it:

---

[3] For a comparison of the reasons given in the Care Plan with those given by social workers, see Chapter 5, para 3.3.

You have to look at what the needs of the child are and try to see how best to meet those needs with the limited resources that you have.

This response neatly expresses the views of many social workers, namely, that aspirations determining the choice of plan were often governed by pragmatic considerations in its execution, particularly in terms of matching the needs of the child with a suitable placement which one social worker felt was sometimes 'a bit of a lottery'.

It is also worth adding that the distinction between adoption and long-term fostering is sometimes bedevilled by muddled thinking about so-called "permanence".[4] In Metro High, for example, the practice was to make decisions on long-term care based on "permanence" (presumably meaning non-rehabilitation) rather than for adoption or long-term fostering. In contrast, in London Low long-term fostering was not seen as a "permanent" status. Similarly, the de facto practice in Shire High was not to treat long-term fostering as a permanent placement.

2 Child-related factors

2.1 Age

The evidence from both the social worker interviews and from the analysis of our Stage 3 data support the view that a key factor in determining whether a child is to be placed for adoption or long-term fostering is the child's age.

Every social worker we interviewed cited age as one of the most crucial factors. The general view was that the younger the child, the more likely adoption would be the preferred option because it had a greater chance of being successful. Older children, it was surmised, had less chance of finding a suitable adoptive family and thus the plan might have to be changed to include the search for a long-term fostering placement. The reasons for this supposition included observations such as older children were more likely to have significant attachments and relationships with their birth families, have a strong identification with and a sense of loyalty

---

[4] See also Chapter 1, para 3.2.

to their birth family, be part of a sibling group and have views about their future (see also Ivaldi, 2000, p. 59). There appeared to be a general consensus on the significant ages influencing the plan:

- For children up to the age of five adoption was the preferred option and was most likely to be successful (London High, Metro High, Shire High), particularly where there had been extreme neglect or abuse and where the need for a permanent home offering stability and constancy was paramount.
- The upper age limit for considering adoption generally ranged from nine to 11 though two of the "Low" authorities suggested between seven and nine as their cut-off age.
- From the age of 10 onwards all the authorities realistically expected the plan to be for long-term fostering. One authority (London High), which had a policy of prioritising adoption for children of all ages, opted for a dual planning approach with long-term fostering after this age. Children over this age could be successfully adopted but suitable placements were more difficult to identify and the risk of disruption was thought to be greater. One team manager from Shire Low maintained that adoption would never be ruled out (i.e. regardless of the child's age) but this particular authority was under pressure to do "better in the adoption stakes".

The importance of the child's age in the planning process was very much reflected in our analysis of the Stage 3 data.

As **Table 14** shows, whereas children aged 1–4 years appear to be twice as likely to have been the subject of a plan for adoption as for long-term fostering, children over the age of five years had less chance of being subject to a plan for adoption with four times as many being the subject of a plan for long-term fostering. For each of the three children in the sample who were aged 10 and over, the plan was for long-term fostering.

Table 14

Age at the start[5] of last episode of being looked after by plan at 31 March 1999

Age at the start of being looked after	Adoption No: %	Long-term fostering No: %	TOTAL No: %
1–4	46 (66%)	24 (34%)	70 (62%)
5–9	8 (20%)	32 (80%)	40 (35%)
10 plus	–	3 (100%)	3 (3%)

Table 15

Age of the child at the start of the last episode of being looked after by plan for the child and local authority

Local authority & plan	1–4	5–9	10 and over	Total cases
London High				
Adoption	6 (55%)	4 (50%)	–	10
Long-term fostering	5 (45%)	4 (50%)	–	9
London Low				
Adoption	8 (67%)	2 (25%)	–	10
Long-term fostering	4 (33%)	6 (75%)	–	10
Metro High				
Adoption	10 (77%)	–	–	10
Long-term fostering	3 (23%)	6 (100%)	1 (100%)	10
Metro Low				
Adoption	10 (67%)	–	–	10
Long-term fostering	5 (33%)	5 (100%)	–	10
Shire High				
Adoption	8 (100%)	2 (20%)	–	10
Long-term fostering	–	8 (80%)	2 (100%)	10
Shire Low				
Adoption	4 (37%)	–	–	4
Long-term fostering	7 (64%)	3 (100%)	–	10

---

[5] This date was thought to be a more useful indicator than age at 31 March 1999 as many of the children in the sample may have been looked after and had their plans ratified for some time prior to this date.

Furthermore, as can be seen in **Table 15** above, the correlation between the age of children at the start of the last episode of being looked after and the plan for them appeared to be stronger in some authorities than others. Age had the least effect on the plan in London High where the children aged 1–4 years and 5–9 years were fairly evenly distributed between plans for adoption and plans for long-term fostering. The strongest correlations between age and plan occurred in Metro High, Metro Low and Shire High. In Metro High and Metro Low there were no children in the sample over the age of five for whom the plan was adoption although there were children under five for whom the plan was long-term fostering. In Shire High none of the children in the sample in the 1–4 years age bracket were the subject of a plan for long-term fostering, although 20 per cent of the children aged 5–9 years were the subject of a plan for adoption. Shire Low seemed to be the only authority that did not follow the general pattern. However, we need to be cautious about drawing too many conclusions since we were only able to collect data on four adoption cases in this authority (see Chapter 1, para 4.5). Nevertheless it is of interest that, while all four were in the 1–4 age group, there were nearly twice as many children aged 1–4 years who had plans for long-term fostering.

The importance of age in long-term planning decisions was further evidenced by our findings concerning the factors social workers provided (both in the interviews and as recorded in the children's case files) as reasons for specific plans they had made for adoption and long-term fostering. In nine of the 17 cases with plans for adoption that social workers were asked about when interviewed, age was stated as a factor in the formulation of the plan and indeed was the factor most frequently mentioned. Age was the second most frequently mentioned factor recorded in the case files of those children for whom the plan was adoption (eight out of 29). In contrast, while age was the second most frequently mentioned factor in relation to those cases where the plan was for long-term fostering (nine out of the 19 long-term fostering cases discussed in interviews), it was only the sixth most common factor recorded in the children's case files.

As we discuss later (see below at para 3.1), the child's age is not un-related to another crucial factor in the planning process, namely, their degree of contact with the birth family.

2.2 Gender

Although not mentioned either in the case files or by social workers in relation to specific cases, the Stage 3 data did nevertheless reveal some overall gender differences in relation to the planned option. We found evidence that, generally, plans for adoption were more likely to be made for girls than boys. In the overall Stage 3 sample, adoption plans had been made for 57 per cent of girls but for only 41 per cent of the boys. The difference was particularly marked in relation to the 1–4 year-old age group in which adoption was planned for 80 per cent of the girls as opposed to 55 per cent of the boys. While gender was barely mentioned as a factor in planning for the child's long-term future, some social workers did refer to it as being influential in executing the plan. It appeared difficult to find a suitable adoptive placement for boys, particularly once they had reached the age of eight. As one social worker commented:

We know that there is a short period that we have, especially for young boys, when we have to get them adopted. If not, then it's almost impossible.

Girls, on the other hand, were thought easier to place for adoption. As one social worker from Metro Low put it:

Girls are easier to get adopted, particularly pretty children, which is very sad but it's a fact.

Another social worker suggested that gender did not so much influence the choice of plan as the choice of placement. He felt that in terms of the matching process there were some cases where boys who had had a poor experience of a father figure needed a placement where the father's role was strong and positive. Similarly girls, where there had been a lack of maternal love and attachment, needed to find a placement with female carers who had the capacity to recognise this and fulfil the child's needs.

2.3 Ethnicity and culture

In three of the authorities, ethnicity and culture were not mentioned as factors which might influence the making of the long-term plan (London High, which has a large multi-ethnic community; Shire High and Metro

High). One social worker in London Low – another multi-ethnic community – said that adoption would be a difficult choice of plan for children from some cultures in which adoption was considered wrong and might induce recriminations against the birth parents.[6]

Although the number of cases is small, the Stage 3 data support the view that ethnicity is a factor in determining whether a child is placed for adoption or long-term fostering. Of the 20 children who were of black minority ethnic origin, or of mixed parentage, 13 were the subject of a plan for long-term fostering (65 per cent).[7] In contrast, children whose parents were white were only slightly more likely to be subject of a plan for adoption (53 per cent) than for long-term fostering (47 per cent).[8]

Ethnicity and culture of the child were mentioned as factors that might cause a plan for adoption to be changed to long-term fostering if no suitable match with adopters could be found. Linked with this might be the problem of the geographical location of a suitable match, especially if the child had specific cultural needs.

In Metro Low, ethnicity was mentioned as a possible determining factor by all three social workers interviewed. They said that it was difficult to find adopters for minority ethnic children because there were very few black and Asian foster carers and, particularly, adopters in their area.[9] Where adoption was thought to be the best plan for a particular child but suitable adopters could not be found to meet that child's ethnic needs, they would probably look at the possibility of making an ethnically appropriate temporary foster placement. One social worker said that

---

[6] The Government have recognised the problem and following the proposals in the White Paper (*Adoption: A new approach* at para 5.8), the Adoption and Children Bill makes provision for special guardianship to provide for "permanence" short of complete legal separation which adoption necessarily involves.

[7] Interestingly, five of the seven minority ethnic children who were subject to a plan for adoption were of mixed parentage. This is in line with Ivaldi's finding that 73% of minority ethnic children adopted out of care were of mixed parentage (see Ivaldi, 2000, at p. 113).

[8] Of 76 children whose parents were both white, 40 (53%) were subject to a plan for adoption and 36 (47%) for long-term fostering. Information was missing on 17 children.

[9] Cf Ivaldi (2000, p. 113), who reported that black and mixed heritage children had to wait significantly longer than white children to be placed for adoption.

placing a minority ethnic child with white adopters, even if they were racially aware, would have difficulties. She did not think that contact alone was sufficient to address the issues around racial and ethnic identity. She therefore believed that children from minority ethnic communities ended up by default in long-term fostering placements, which may have met their racial and cultural needs but not necessarily their permanency and stability needs.[10]

Two social workers in London Low stressed the importance of placing children with carers from within their own ethnic and cultural group but admitted that the lack of carers within particular cultures might affect whether a plan could be adhered to.

2.4 Emotional and behavioural problems and other special needs

Both our Stage 3 data and the evidence from the social worker interviews show that another key factor determining whether a child is to be placed for adoption or long-term fostering concerns the child's emotional and behavioural problems and other special needs. Examining the planning decisions for specific cases recorded by social workers in case files or provided in the interviews, we found that children with emotional and behavioural problems were more likely to be subject to plans for long-term fostering than for adoption.

Caution needs to be exercised in interpreting this evidence since it is likely that social workers used varying definitions of emotional and behavioural problems and because the case files seldom gave any indication as to the severity of the conditions.[11]

---

[10] Note: the issue of transracial adoptions was considered in the White Paper. At para 6.15 it is suggested that: 'All councils should be proactive in monitoring their local population of looked after children to enable them to recruit permanent carers who can meet their needs. However, the child's welfare is paramount, and no child should be denied loving adoptive parents solely on the grounds that the child and the parents do not share the same racial or cultural background.'

[11] For this reason we decided against attempting to correlate these conditions by gender and age of the children lest to do so would ascribe or suggest a degree of precision which the quality of the data did not justify.

Table 16

Evidence of emotional or behavioural conditions by the plan for the child

Evidence of emotional or behavioural conditions	Adoption No: %	Long-term fostering No: %	TOTAL No: %
Yes	15 (36%)	27 (64%)	42 (100%)
No	39 (55%)	32 (45%)	71 (100%)

In 42 out of the 113 case files in our Stage 3 sample, it was stated that there was evidence of the child having emotional or behavioural difficulties (37%). In London High and Shire High, over half the children were said to be in this category, although in Metro High there were only three such cases (15%). Although we cannot tell from these data how severe these problems were, as can be seen from **Table 16** above, for a higher percentage of children (two-thirds) with emotional or behavioural difficulties the plan was for long-term fostering rather than for adoption (one-third). However, when analysed by authority, the position became more complicated. In Metro High, for instance, the pattern was reversed with one-third of the children having a plan for long-term fostering and two-thirds having a plan for adoption. However, as stated above, there were only three children in this authority where there was evidence of emotional or behavioural difficulties and therefore conclusions should not be drawn. In Shire Low, the children with evidence of emotional or behavioural difficulties were equally split between plans for adoption and plans for long-term fostering, whereas in Metro Low there were no children with evidence of emotional or behavioural difficulties with plans for adoption.

Most of the social workers we interviewed said that they were more likely to consider long-term fostering than adoption for children with emotional and behavioural problems. In three of the authorities, a child's ability to form attachments was considered significant in determining the plan. The younger the child, the greater his or her chances were considered to be of forming attachments with an adoptive family. Some of the social workers in Metro High and Metro Low thought that, if a child was going to have difficulty forming attachments or had behavioural problems, they would be more likely to choose long-term fostering as the plan because:

- It was difficult to identify adoptive placements that could meet these children's needs. One social worker felt that, even with children as young as four years old – 'normally a good adoptable age' – there was a danger of them being 'set up to fail' because adopters needed 'to be accepted by the children and to save kids who have been in care'.
- They would be reluctant to place such a child in an adoptive placement with a high risk of disruption.
- Foster carers were more likely to know how to gain access to the appropriate resources and professionals to help and support them in managing the placement. While theoretically, such services and support were also available to adopters, one of the social workers, reflecting a commonly-held view, told us that, because of their lack of experience and lack of ongoing contact with social services, adopters were less knowledgeable about what resources they needed, what was available and how to obtain them.

Another social worker said that adoption was not usually the best option for children with behavioural and attachment problems, especially those who had been sexually or physically abused, due to the lack of post-adoption support. She said that she would be mindful of whether adoptive parents would be able to cope and invest enough in the child to make the placement work. It was also suggested by a different social worker that it might be difficult to find an adoptive placement for a child with a physical disability, especially if there were no support from social services. She did, however, add that long-term foster placements were no easier to find in such cases, but at least the carers were given some support. Another reason given for the choice of long-term fostering for children with emotional or behavioural difficulties was the possibility of continuing support available to carers in the form of respite care and a residential placement – support which might not be available for adoptive families.

Although the above stated evidence clearly demonstrates the importance of taking into account the child's emotional or behavioural difficulties when determining what long-term option should be chosen, many of the above mentioned reasons for preferring long-term fostering over adoption seem weak. In particular, the lack of support for adopters as against that for foster carers seems hard to justify. Even harder to justify is the notion that foster carers find it easier than adopters to gain access to vital support resources and professional help. In these respects, is it not the local authority's responsibility to ensure that adequate support is both available and is known about?

Whether foster carers are better able to handle the undoubted strain and stress of looking after emotionally disturbed children is an interesting question. It may be that unlike adopters, who could well have an intense need for attachment, well-trained "professional" foster carers are better able to take on this difficult task, but whether this is well thought through by local authorities is open to question. There is certainly a danger that short-term rather than long-term solutions are being found to look after such children.[12]

2.5   Evidence of abuse

Where it was recorded in case files, information was collected on the four different categories of abuse, namely, sexual, emotional, physical and neglect. Neglect was the most frequently reported in half of the cases (N = 56, 50%); followed by emotional abuse (N = 42, 37%); physical abuse (N = 32, 28%) and finally sexual abuse in 16 cases (14%). As in the case of the evidence of emotional and behavioural problems (see para 2.4 above), we should enter the caveat that the definition of abuse is relatively "soft" in as much as the case files seldom detail its extent or severity or even whether the abuse was merely suspected or proved.

Given the limited number of cases where the individual forms of abuse were found, it was decided to count the number of different categories of abuse recorded for each child in order to produce an overall summary of

---

[12] The Government has sought to address the problem of children lingering in care by establishing (following the proposal made in the Adoption White Paper, ibid, at para 4.6) national adoption standards (see *National Adoption Standards for England*, Department of Health, 2001). These standards, which will come into force from 1 April 2003 (see LAC (2002) 33 (though note the Standards for Wales have not yet been finalised), provide timescales within which decisions for most children will be reached and action taken. Furthermore, it is intended that these standards will make provision for a comprehensive package of post-placement and post-adoption support.

their prevalence. Thus, as **Table 17** below shows, no evidence of abuse was recorded in just over one-quarter of the case files, with a third recording only one count of abuse and a further quarter two counts. Three-quarters of the evidence of neglect was found in the case files recording only one or two types of abuse, as was 71 per cent of the evidence of emotional abuse. Physical abuse was mostly to be found among the case files recording two or three different types of abuse. Finally, sexual abuse was evenly distributed, with four cases being found in each category.

It is also interesting to note that the recording of two or three different types of abuse rose according to the age of the child, from 13 per cent of those aged 1–4 to 40 per cent of those aged 5–9 and 45 per cent of those aged between 10 and 12.

Table 17
Evidence of abuse by the plan for the child

Evidence of abuse	Adoption No: %	Long-term fostering No: %	TOTAL No: %
None	17 (57%)	13 (43%)	30 (100%)
One type	20 (51%)	19 (49%)	39 (100%)
Two types	12 (41%)	17 (59%)	29 (100%)
Three types	3 (27%)	8 (73%)	11 (100%)
All four types	2 (50%)	2 (50%)	4 (100%)

Table 17 above also shows the differences in the amount of evidence of abuse by the plan for the child. It can be seen that children with none, or only one type of abuse listed (which as noted above is most likely to be neglect or emotional abuse) were slightly more likely to be subject to a plan for adoption. Children with evidence of two or three different types of abuse noted in their case files were more likely to be subject to a plan for long-term fostering. There was no difference, however, when evidence of all four types of abuse was present in the case files.

2.6 The child's wishes

Another child-related factor of potential importance is the child's own wishes. Given that this factor is likely to be of increasing importance the older the child is, it is worth bearing in mind that in our sample all the children were below the age of 13.

We report first on the evidence from the social work interviews. In three authorities (Shire Low, Shire High and Metro High), the child's views were considered to be an important factor affecting the choice of long-term plan,[13] particularly in association with the child's age, their level of contact and their relationship with their birth family. Children were not being asked to make the decision, but their views would be taken into account. As one team leader in Metro High said, although they should listen to the child's views, it was their responsibility to make a decision based on the child's needs and not simply to follow what a child might want. Some children, if asked, would probably say that they wanted to live at home, which might not be in their best interests.

The relative importance of the child's wishes as a factor in formulating plans for adoption and long-term fostering was further borne out in the reasons recorded in the case files and provided by the social workers we interviewed when asked about specific cases in our Stage 3 sample. In fact the child's wishes was respectively the third and fourth most frequently stated reason for long-term fostering and adoption as recorded on the case files and the equal fourth and third most frequently stated reason respectively for long-term fostering and adoption given by social workers in interviews.

So far as the Stage 3 data are concerned, we found that in one-third of the case files examined, there was evidence that the views of the child had been taken into consideration (N = 36, 32%). In 43 per cent of the case files, it was stated that the child was "too young" to express an

---

[13] Interestingly, in London Low children's wishes were not mentioned as a significant factor by any of the social workers interviewed. Cf the *National Adoption Standards for England*, op cit, at A4, which states 'Every child will have his or her wishes or feelings listened to, recorded and taken into account. Where they are not acted upon, the reasons for doing or not doing so will be explained to the child and properly recorded.'

opinion or had a disability which would make it impossible for them to understand or comment sufficiently (N = 49).[14] In the remaining quarter of the files, there was no evidence on file that the child's views had been taken into account (N = 28). In 21 of these cases the plan was for long-term fostering.

In 16 cases, the child was stated to be happy with his or her placement (12 of which were long-term foster placements), and in nine cases, it was stated that the plan had been explained to the child (eight were for long-term foster care).

In nine cases, the actual wishes of the child were recorded, two having attended the review meeting to state their wish to be adopted. In two other cases, although the children had expressed their views against being placed for adoption, adoption remained the plan. Conversely, in another case, in which long-term fostering was the plan, the child had expressed the view that he/she did not wish to be adopted as there was still a strong bond with his/her family.

3 Family-related factors

3.1 Child's relationship/contact with their birth family

Linked with age, the child's relationship and level of contact with his or her birth parents and extended family members (including siblings and grandparents) was considered to be a crucial factor by all the social workers interviewed in deciding whether the long-term plan should be adoption or long-term fostering. They generally stated that the older the child, the more significant the relationship with their birth family was likely to be and, therefore, the greater the probability that the chosen plan would be long-term fostering. Furthermore, when social workers were interviewed about specific cases from the Stage 3 sample, contact with the birth family emerged as a key factor in long-term planning decisions. This was mirrored in the reasons for care plans that social workers recorded in case files. Maintaining contact with the birth family was the

---

[14] It was not possible to extract from the data precisely what age "too young" referred to and consequently on whether definition of the term varied between authorities.

most frequently given reason for plans for long-term fostering being stated as a factor in 11 out of 19 cases by the social workers interviewed. Maintaining contact with family was the third most frequently recorded factor in the case files affecting plans for long-term fostering.

The relationship between contact and plans for adoption was also strong, although not as marked as for long-term fostering. Poor, little or no contact with the birth family was given as a reason for the plan by social workers in the interviews in five of the 17 adoption cases, making it the third most frequently given factor along with the child's wishes. At first sight this general view seems to be supported by the Stage 3 data.

Contact with the birth mother

Table 18

Age of the child at the start of being looked after, by plan for the child and existence of contact with birth mother at 31 March 1999

Existence of contact and plan	*1–4* *No: %*	*5–9* *No: %*	*10 and over* *No: %*	*Total cases* *No: %*
Direct				
Adoption	7 (41%)	4 (15%)	–	11 (24%)
Long-term fostering	10 (59%)	23 (85%)	2 (100%)	35 (76%)
Total	17 (37%)	27 (59%)	2 (4%)	46 (100%)
None / Indirect[15]				
Adoption	39 (74%)	4 (31%)	–	43 (64%)
Long-term fostering	14 (26%)	9 (69%)	1 (100%)	24 (35%)
Total	53 (79%)	13 (19%)	1 (1%)	67 (100%)

Table 18 above shows that, overall for children who were in direct contact with their birth mother at 31 March 1999, the plan generally was for their long-term fostering, whereas for those who had indirect or no contact the plan generally was for their adoption.

---

[15] For ease of analysis indirect contact has been combined with no contact. There were only 12 recorded cases of indirect contact which followed the same pattern as for no contact.

When the age of the child is also considered, for the majority of children aged 5–9 years who had direct contact with their birth mother the plan was for long-term fostering. For the majority of children under five years old who did not have such contact, adoption was the plan. This is what one would expect if contact is taken to be an influencing factor. However, what is of interest is that for 69 per cent of the children aged 5–9 years who did not have direct contact with their birth mother, the plan was for long-term fostering. For 41 per cent of the children aged under five, the plan was for adoption even though they had direct contact. In other words, irrespective of whether they had contact with their birth mother, the plan for older children was more likely to be for long-term fostering whereas for younger children the plan was more likely to be for adoption. In short, age seemed to be more important than contact. Additionally, it may be noted that it was anecdotally evident from the case histories that, for some children for whom adoption was the plan, direct contact would subsequently have been phased out nearer to the adoption hearing.

Table 19
Plan for the child and existence of contact with birth mother at 31 March 1999 by local authority

| Local authority | Direct contact | | None/Indirect | |
	Adoption No: %	Long-term fostering No: %	Adoption No: %	Long-term fostering No: %
London High	2 (33%)	4 (67%)	8 (62%)	5 (39%)
London Low	4 (44%)	5 (56%)	6 (55%)	5 (46%)
Metro High	2 (20%)	8 (80%)	8 (80%)	2 (20%)
Metro Low	1 (17%)	5 (83%)	9 (64%)	5 (36%)
Shire High	2 (22%)	7 (78%)	8 (73%)	3 (27%)
Shire Low	–	6 (100%)	4 (50%)	4 (50%)

Analysing the relationship between contact and the plan for the child by local authority, it can be seen from **Table 19** above that in Shire Low for all the children who had direct contact with their birth mothers the plan was for long-term fostering though in this case the numbers were small (i.e. six cases). The authority in which there appeared to be the most direct relationship between contact and the plan for the child was Metro High. Of the children who had direct contact with the birth mother, for 20 per cent the plan was adoption and for 80 per cent the plan was long-term fostering. The authorities with the weakest relationship between contact and the plan for the child were the two London authorities. In London Low, for example, there appeared to be almost no relationship. Of the children who had direct contact with the birth mother, for 44 per cent the plan was adoption and for 56 per cent the plan was long-term fostering. Of the children who had no or little contact with the birth mother, for 55 per cent the plan was adoption and for 46 per cent the plan was long-term fostering.

Contact with the birth father

Table 20
Plan for the child and existence of contact with birth father at 31 March 1999

Contact with birth father	Adoption No: %	Long-term fostering No: %	TOTAL No: %
Direct contact	5 (26%)	14 (74%)	19 (17%)
None or indirect contact	49 (52%)	45 (48%)	94 (83%)

For children who had direct contact with their birth fathers the plan was also far more likely to be long-term fostering (74%), with only a quarter being planned for adoption. On the other hand, having no or indirect contact with the birth father appeared to have little effect on the plan for the child, with almost half of the children in this category having a plan for adoption and just over half having a plan for long-term fostering. The less significant effect of an absence of contact with the birth father on the plan could be partially explained by the fact that many children in this category were not having contact with their fathers prior to be being looked after. In other words, the father was absent.

Contact with other family members

The Stage 3 data revealed that just over one-third of the children in the sample were still in contact with other family members at 31 March 1999 (N = 39, 35%). Most frequently mentioned were grandparents, with 15 children being in contact with their maternal grandmother (38%). In five case files contact was recorded with stepfathers, maternal aunts and the extended family generally.

When the existence of contact is examined in relation to the plan for the child, it can be seen from **Table 21** below that, for two-thirds of the children who remained in contact with their other family members, the plan was for long-term fostering, compared with a third of those for whom the plan was adoption.

Table 21
Contact with other family members as at 31 March 1999 analysed by plan for the child

Contact with other family members	Adoption No: %	Long-term fostering No: %	TOTAL No: %
Yes	13 (33%)	26 (67%)	39 (35%)
None	41 (55%)	33 (45%)	74 (65%)

Issues of rehabilitation

Notwithstanding an awareness that long-term fostering held no guarantee of permanency, social workers considered it to be the preferred option where there was still a chance of rehabilitation, even if this was not expected to occur in the immediate future. Where the child was old enough to have and maintain a relationship with members of the birth family, especially the birth father or mother, adoption was generally regarded to be too final an option. Children's identity and loyalty to their birth family were also considered important factors in precluding adoption. As one social worker commented:

They can be happy in a foster placement because they know it's a foster family, they still have their family and their surname.

Another, referring to a specific case, told us:

> *The boys have actually said they want to be adopted but they also know that it would be incredibly difficult to tell their grandparents and mother... We weren't sure what kind of effect it would have on them long term because although they are not closely attached there is something about knowing they are there and knowing who their extended family is.*

Social workers in Metro High thought that parents who were not able to meet the day-to-day needs of the child for whatever reason could still have a relationship with them and offer important emotional support and consistency in terms of the relationship. They felt that, even if contact took place only once or twice a year, it was worth maintaining and they were therefore more likely to choose long-term fostering.

In Shire High, it was possible to detect a pattern among the cases where adoption was favoured over long-term fostering, namely:

- where rehabilitation had been tried and had failed;
- where the birth family could not co-operate with the plans for rehabilitation;
- where there was no foreseeable way back for the child into the birth family, either because of abuse or severe neglect.

Long-term foster care was the preferred option when there was an ongoing relationship with a high level of contact (i.e. weekly) between the child and at least one of the birth parents.

Adoption with contact

In the majority of cases, contact had a greater influence on the choice of plan for older children but, as social workers in Metro Low pointed out, sometimes younger children had strong enough attachments to rule out adoption. Alternatively, adoption was sometimes considered for *older* children who did not have strong attachments to their birth families.

Social workers thought that it was easier to recruit adopters for children where there was little or no contact with their birth family. It also enabled the children to have a "fresh start" in life. A view that was generally shared by social workers was that usually adoptive placements would be ruled out if there was any contact taking place because: first, adoptive carers, for the most part, were unwilling to facilitate or cope with contact, and secondly, there was no guarantee that, once they had parental responsibility, adopters would maintain contact.

> *If there was a way that, after adoption, you could still have some level of control in terms of contact issues and ongoing identity, I may view things differently.*

A team manager suggested that:

> *The ideal would be if we could look at adoptive families taking children and maintaining a high level of contact that is appropriate for that child, but finding adopters that are willing to be as open as that is hard. That would make a difference in terms of adoption and long-term fostering.*

Social workers generally gave the impression that, although they favoured direct post-adoption contact in appropriate cases with parents, siblings or other extended birth family members in theory, they had found it hard to make it work in practice. This was partly due to the difficulties of finding potential adopters who were willing to facilitate contact, and partly due to adopters being unable to cope with the reality, even if they agreed in principle, to contact taking place. One social worker suggested that they were more likely to agree to sibling contact. However, another social worker described the difficulties of implementing a contact agreement in a case where three different families had adopted four siblings:

> *They [i.e. the adoptive parents] found the reality very different from their expectation, even to a degree that the adoptive families couldn't agree when letterbox contact with mum should happen. You could see their own needs to parent the child coming in and, to a degree, overriding what we were saying were the needs of the child.*

Adoption with contact was being encouraged in London Low, although social workers were having problems finding families willing to accept it. Two cases had been considerably delayed as a result, and the plan had had to be changed to long-term fostering. One social worker did, however, acknowledge that with 'an incredible amount of work and support and services', it might eventually be possible to get adoptive families to accept direct contact.[16]

3.2 The extended family as carers

In all six authorities, extended family members were always considered as carers once rehabilitation to the birth parents had been ruled out. The availability of relative carers was not necessarily a factor which affected the choice of plan in terms of adoption or long-term fostering, although one social worker said that in their authority they were considered because of the lack of fostering placements.

If extended family members were willing to look after the child and were assessed as suitable so to do, their status as carers would be determined by the type and extent of support they might need. In Metro Low and Metro High, they preferred family members not to have the status of approved foster carers because it was thought better for the child if there were no social services involvement. Grandparents, for example, were more likely to be approved as foster carers only if difficulties were anticipated about contact with the birth parents or if they needed financial assistance. In Shire Low and London Low, where there were large numbers of children living with grandparents, social workers encouraged family carers to seek a residence order. In London High, involving the extended family was a new development. There was some concern over fostering

---

[16] The White Paper (ibid, at para 6.43) proposed that the National Adoption Standards should state that the child's links with their birth family should always be considered and that, where appropriate, the local authority should make arrangements to meet those needs of the child. *The National Adoption Standards for England*, op cit, at A10 and 11 and C4, now respectively provide: 'The child's needs, wishes and feelings, and their welfare and safety are the most important concerns when considering links or contact with birth parents, with birth family members or other people who are significant to them.'

'Adoption plans will include details of the arrangements for maintaining links (including contact) with birth parents, wider birth family members and other people who are significant to the child and how and when these arrangements will be reviewed.'

'Adoptive parents will be involved in discussions as to how they can best maintain any links, including contact, with birth relatives and significant others identified in the birth plan.'

allowances, especially as social workers thought that family members might not meet the criteria of the local authority for being approved as foster carers and would therefore not receive the larger allowance.[17]

3.3 Attachment to carers

The most frequently cited reasons for deciding on long-term fostering recorded in case files by social workers were related to the child remaining with the current carer, including attachment issues. Thirteen of the files in which clear reasons were given for plans for long-term fostering recorded this factor.

Social workers in both Metro High and Metro Low raised the relationship of carer and child as an important factor in long-term planning, particularly in relation to short-term foster carers wanting to become long-term carers. Social workers from several authorities also talked about children being adopted by long-term foster carers. This was sometimes referred to as planning "by default".[18] A child could spend a long time in what was originally intended as a short-term placement while birth parents were assessed or care proceedings were being pursued. One social worker said that attachment would be taken into account, especially for a particularly vulnerable child who had significant needs and/or had previously experienced difficulties in staying in placements. If a placement was working well for a vulnerable child it could be very counter-productive to disrupt it. Other social workers cited cases where children remained in long-term foster care, even though the plan was for adoption because the child was happy, or because the carers and child wished it.

---

[17] For further discussion on policy and support for extended families as carers, see para 4.6 below and Chapter 5, p. 114.

[18] Following the proposal in the White Paper (ibid, at para 5.7) that 'where a foster carer wants to adopt the child in their care, and that adoption would be in the interests of the child, the foster carer's application should be received positively and processed in three months . . .' the *National Adoption Standards for England* op cit, at 135 states 'Foster carers who make a formal application to adopt children in their care will be entitled to the same information and preparation as other adopters and be assessed within four months.' Hopefully, this may help local authorities to see adoption by foster carers in a more positive light.

In one of the sample cases in Metro High, a team leader explained that it had been decided that the child should stay with her current carers though whether on the basis of adoption or long-term fostering had still to be determined. He commented that:

The foster parents' request to adopt influenced the decision because if the present carers hadn't put themselves in the frame we would probably have gone down the route of maintaining them in that placement on a long-term fostering basis.

He added that he thought it would have been preferable for the child and her sister to stay together with the same carers on a long-term fostering basis rather than to have been adopted by different carers.

3.4 Sibling groups

No clear picture emerged from either our Stage 3 data or from our social worker interviews as to whether being part of a sibling group generally affected long-term planning. To some extent the plan was governed by the ages of the children within the sibling group, by the strength of attachment between the siblings and by the needs of the other siblings.

In Metro High, keeping sibling groups together was considered to play an important role in the preservation of the children's sense of identity. Social workers preferred, where possible, to keep sibling groups together or, at the very least to maintain contact between them. In two authorities the social workers said that if attachments between siblings were strong then long-term fostering would be the more likely plan to enable them to stay together, presumably because it was more difficult to place sibling groups together for adoption. However, younger children were often found adoptive placements while older ones were placed for long-term fostering. It was suggested that older siblings found such situations more difficult to cope with than the younger ones who had been adopted. There was also no guarantee that contact between the siblings would be maintained. It was also pointed out that young children who were not having contact with their birth family were often hard to place for adoption if they had contact with older siblings in long-term fostering placements, as this created an indirect link between the adopters and the birth family.

A social worker in Metro Low suggested that one of the reasons that might militate against finding an adoptive placement for siblings of varying ages was that potential adopters stated what age group they wanted on the application forms. Consequently this made it harder to identify adopters who were willing to take children from different age categories. In Shire Low being part of a sibling group was not thought to be a factor that influenced the choice of plan. Because this shire county had a high number of large sibling groups (one social worker talked about a family of eight she had had to find placements for), it was as difficult to find a fostering family to take on three or four children at a time, as it was to find an adoptive family.

3.5 Summary

Previously, three principal factors from the Stage 3 data were identified as having an influence on the decision-making process, namely the age of the child, their gender, and the amount of contact which they retained with their birth family, principally their birth mother.

It has been shown that younger children, especially the under-fives, were more likely to be subject to a plan for adoption. Girls, particularly younger girls, were similarly more likely to be subject to a plan for adoption. Finally, children who were in direct contact with their birth mothers were more likely to have a plan for long-term fostering, and those who had only indirect contact, or no contact, were more likely to have a plan for adoption.

These three variables were analysed using a simple logistic regression, in order to assess their interaction.[19] It was found that there

[19] *Table 22* **Results of logistic regression model predicting adoption**

	Odds ratio	95% Confidence interval	p-value
Gender	21.9	(2.32, 205.85)	0.007
Age	0.8	(0.70, 0.99)	0.038
Age by Gender	0.6	(0.34, 0.89)	0.016
Contact	0.4	(0.17, 1.06)	0.065

The logistic regression model was constructed using the age at the start of being looked after and contact with the birth mother at 31 March 1999. The way in which the research project was constructed meant that contact at the start of being looked after, or when the plan was made, was not recorded. Whilst information was collected on the date at which the plan was made, this was subject to error, and could subsequently not be relied upon to calculate the age at which the plan was made. Had these other indicators been available, the model is likely to have been even more predictive.

was a highly significant increase in probability of adoption for girls. Older children were less likely to have plans for adoption, with a reduction of 20 per cent in their odds for each year older they were at the start of being looked after. There was also a significant interaction between age and gender, indicating that the effect of gender is modified in older children, with a greater reduction in probability of adoption for girls as they get older. Finally, contact with the birth mother had only border-line significance when the other variables in the model were taken into account.

4 Organisational-related factors

We presented social workers with a list of organisational-related factors which might have an influence on the choice of plan and asked them to comment on which, if any, were important.

4.1 Policies

In this section we consider whether social workers were aware of depart-mental policies that may influence their choice of plan. From the social workers' interviews it was evident that certain authorities had clear specific policies advocating adoption.

As already mentioned (see para 2.1 above), London High had a policy of always planning for adoption regardless of the age of the child or any special needs he or she may have had. If no suitable adoptive family could be found after a certain length of time, the plan might be changed to include long-term fostering as an alternative "second-best" placement. In London Low, the social workers were also very clear that adoption was the best option when the child could not return home.

In Shire Low, all the social workers interviewed were aware of the newly developed, clearly written policies on adoption and permanence. The authority had recently been criticised for their poor adoption rate and senior managers were keen to raise the profile of adoption in social workers' planning for the long-term care of a child. However, it appeared from interviews with social workers that, although they approved of the new policies, it was likely to be some time before old working practices would be overcome.

In Shire High, their published guidelines were considered very carefully by social workers before making an assessment about the long-term care of a child. Although this authority had a high adoption rate, its focus was on ensuring that all looked after children had a plan which was regularly monitored without particularly promoting one long-term option over another.

4.2   Individual "team working" practices[20]

In two of the sample authorities, Shire Low and Metro Low, it was suggested to us at the reconnaissance interview with senior managers that individual "team-working" practices might be contributing to a significant variation between teams and areas in the number of children being adopted or fostered long-term. Accordingly, the possibility that there were particular team policies in relation to the choice of long-term plans was presented to social workers in the list of organisational-related factors referred to above.

None of the social workers in either of the aforementioned authorities identified this as a relevant factor. However, in Metro Low, we had sufficient cases from the different area teams to examine whether such a difference existed. We found that there was variation in the teams' use of adoption and long-term fostering according to the plan for the child at 31 March 1999 for those in the Stage 2 sample. This authority has been reorganised since then, so we are only able to say that under the former set-up the suspicions of the senior managers would appear to have been justified. The Director, in a subsequent interview, confirmed that there had been some problems with consistency in long-term planning. It was felt that the teams were too scattered and autonomous and that the views of the team leaders were having more influence than those of the department. In Shire Low, there were so few adoptions at the time covered by our data collection that we were unable to establish the existence of any team differences.

In another authority, one of the team managers said that, because of his strong personal belief in adoption, he always strongly advocated that choice of plan for younger children to the social workers in his team. A

---

[20] See also Chapter 5, para 2.3.

second team manager in the same area was more equivocal, her focus being the avoidance of drift and delay and dealing with the reality of what was possible.

Social workers and managers in the other three authorities were not aware of any individual team practices in relation to the choice of a long-term plan, although one team manager in Shire High thought that each area in the county had a slightly different culture, which might prompt small variations in practice. There is a possibility that differences in decision-making for long-term planning may exist, not only between individual teams, but between individual social workers. In this research, we have not had the time to examine these particular aspects of potential influence on long-term planning.

4.3 Timing of the planning

One social worker raised concerns about the effect that the timing of long-term planning might have on the choice of plan. A team manager from Shire High explained how essential it was for adoption to be considered as a choice early in the discussion, otherwise there was a danger of "missing the boat" because the longer contact continued with the birth family, the more difficult it might be to choose adoption as the long-term plan.[21]

---

[21] It is to be noted that, following the proposal in the White Paper (ibid, at paras 4.6 and 5.17), a key part of the *National Adoption Standards for England* is the establishment of timescales which includes the production of a plan for permanence for all looked after children at the four month statutory review, and where adoption has been identified as the plan for the child at a review, the adoption panel will make its decision within two months and a meeting with suitable adoptive parents will be identified and approved by the panel within six months of the agency agreeing that adoption is in the child's best interests. For our findings on timing, see Chapter 4.

4.4   Availability of adopters and foster carers

Availability

Social workers were asked whether they considered that the availability of adopters and foster carers was a factor in influencing the outcome of the plan.

The social workers in both London authorities said that, although there was a scarcity of adopters and long-term foster carers within their boundaries, they had no problems finding placements outside the local authority area, some in the home counties, some as far away as Sheffield or Norfolk, and one even on a Caribbean island. London authorities had a mixed population of long-established cultural groups and newly-arrived asylum seekers from many different parts of the world. The difficulty of placing children locally meant that the need to find a placement sometimes took precedence over cultural concerns and, as a result, children often had to be placed out of their local community.

The two Metropolitan authorities appeared to suffer from a scarcity of both adopters and long-term foster carers. Similarly in Shire High, social workers noted more than once that there was a paucity of suitable resources, especially long-term foster carers. On the other hand, social workers in Shire Low said that they had not experienced any difficulties in finding adoptive families for children under the age of six years within the county boundaries, though for children above this age the position was not so straightforward.[22]

Overall, therefore, in our six authorities, the evidence from the social workers suggests that there was a mixed picture of availability of adopters and long-term foster carers which makes generalisations hazardous.

Consequences of lack of availability

Social workers in Metro Low maintained that the lack of adopters or foster carers would not affect the initial decision-making but that it might

---

[22] Though it will be noted we found very few adoptions in this authority.

be a factor in executing the plan.[23] If a carer had not been found within a certain time, they would consider changing the plan, usually from adoption to long-term fostering. One social worker in Metro Low said that, if she thought adoption was the appropriate plan for a child but that it was unlikely that adopters would be found, she would still present her plan to the court stating that, although she thought adoption was in the best interests of the child, reality dictated that they would probably be looking for a long-term fostering placement. Another said that, if she thought it was going to be difficult to find adopters, she would not plan for adoption even if she thought that adoption was in the best interests of the child.

One reason social workers gave for changing the plan was the damaging effect that delay in finding an adoptive placement might have on the self-esteem of the children, making them feel negative about themselves and rejected. There was a need to weigh up the ideal plan of an adoptive placement against the damage children might suffer by waiting. As one social worker put it:

> *There is a dilemma. For example, if you've got a girl in a residential unit and you're finding it difficult to find adopters for her, how long do you wait until you've found what she really needs, or should you start looking for a long-term fostering placement because at least she'd be in a family and not in a residential unit? Do we wait until we find what's perfect or do we try and give her something that's better than she's got now?*

An important consequence of the scarcity of long-term fostering placements was that children for whom the plan was long-term fostering were often lingering in a holding placement until a suitable placement was found.

---

[23] Following the White Paper's proposal, op cit at para 4.6, *The National Adoption Standards for England,* op cit at F6, states: 'Agencies will plan, implement and evaluate effective strategies to recruit sufficient adopters and meet the needs of children waiting for adoption locally and nationally especially those from diverse ethnic and cultural backgrounds and disabled children.' To help this process, and again following the White Paper's proposals, op cit at para 6.7, a new Adoption Register for England and Wales has been established to enable adoption agencies to match children with potential adopters.

Social workers in Metro Low also talked about how availability of long-term foster carers or adopters influenced whether they took children away from the birth family in the first place, thereby raising the threshold level of risk they were willing to accept. As one said:

We end up managing incredibly risky situations that perhaps we wouldn't be managing in the community if we had the families available . . . If the alternative is small children, six, seven and eight year-old children coming into residential units . . . then we'll live with a very much higher level of risk than maybe we would have once.

Partly because of the quality of care in residential units and the risk to children of being bullied and abused in residential care, one social worker said that, unless there was a "really good reason", she would be trying to rehabilitate the children. This social worker also expressed concern about the quality of foster placements.

Difficulties in placing children with special needs

There are some children (for example, those with special needs such as ill-health, disability or emotional or behavioural difficulties) for whom it was especially difficult to find adopters.[24] One team manager in London said that social workers had to be constantly pragmatic in their search for a long-term placement for a child, particularly if that child was over a certain age (usually 10 years old), part of a sibling group, or from a culture in which adoption was frowned upon. A social worker in Shire High said that it was also difficult to place children for adoption whose parents had a history of chronic mental health problems because of the fear that these problems may be inherited. Children with severe emotional or behavioural problems were similarly difficult to place. In fact, several social workers said that it was the uncertainty both about the past and the future which made some potential adoptive carers wary of "taking on" such children. They were more likely to "take on" children with physical disabilities because there was sufficient information, advice and support groups in place and because they knew what difficulties they were likely to face in the future.

---

[24] See also the discussion at para 2.4.

This last comment also gives an indication of one of the factors which social workers believed has a significant influence on whether people choose to become long-term foster carers or adopters, namely, the extent of support that social services are able to give, both in financial and social work terms. This is the subject of the next two sections.

4.5   Budgetary constraints and allowances[25]

Budgetary constraints were mentioned directly by only three social workers (all from Metro Low) as being an influential factor in their decision-making, principally because they were unable to use foster carers from outside agencies due to their higher cost. A team manager in another authority stated that at every review meeting they were constantly being reminded about budgets and consequently, while they quite often started by looking at what the child needed, they ended up with a compromise in terms of what was in the "pot". Another social worker felt that such restraints were increasingly becoming a factor, much to his team's frustration and annoyance.

One social worker gave a different type of example where she thought budgetary constraints were playing a significant role. This concerned children who were in a placement with private agency carers. She cited the example of a couple who wished to look after the children long-term but the department was not prepared to pay the high placement costs. She had been told that, if the children were to stay there, she had to persuade the carers either to adopt them or become local authority foster carers which would have involved asking the couple to accept a substantial drop in income of maybe £250 per week.

Allowances for adoption and long-term fostering[26]

Although social workers in authorities other than Metro Low did not mention budgetary constraints directly, it was clear from their comments that they attributed the unwillingness of, for example, some long-term foster carers to become adoptive carers, or short-term carers to become

---

[25] See also the discussion in Chapter 5 at para 2.2.
[26] See also the discussion in the White Paper, op cit, at paras 6.32–6.36.

long-term carers, to the different rates in allowances paid by their local authority. Because of the effect that this might have on the availability of long-term foster carers or adopters, this in turn might influence the outcome of the chosen plan.

One social worker felt that, because it was acceptable for married women to work rather than stay at home and care for the family, long-term fostering was now regarded more as an occupation which needed to be suitably rewarded. Echoing this, another thought that the fostering service had never 'really caught up with the fact that women work'.

Although we did not investigate the different rates given for each allowance in each authority, it became clear through the comments of social workers that these varied sometimes quite substantially.[27] One social worker's awareness of this arose from her experience of placing children outside her own county in areas where fostering rates were much more generous.

One team manager in London High said that if short-term foster carers wished to care for a child on a long-term basis, they were more likely to choose long-term fostering than adoption because of the level of payments. As a result, the plan would have to be changed to accommodate this preference. Similarly, in London Low, a social worker said that the adoption panel should consider granting generous adoption allowances in cases where long-term foster carers wished to adopt a child, if adoption was the preferred plan. In some authorities, adoption allowances were increased if the child had special needs. One social worker in London High thought that the shortage of long-term foster carers in her area could be due to financial restrictions. A short-term foster carer was paid a

---

[27] Fostering Network publish a yearly survey of fostering allowances. However, since we are pledged not to publish details which could identify the local authorities studied we will not comment further about specifics. Since completing our study there has been an interesting decision on the legality of differential rates, namely, *The Queen on the Application of L and Others v Manchester City Council; The Queen on the Application of R and Another v Manchester City Council* [2001] EWHC Admin 707, [2002] 1 FLR 43 in which it was held to be unlawful to pay short-term foster carers who were friends or relatives of the child a lower rate that that paid to other foster carers. For a discussion of the varying rates of adoption allowances as found in previous research, see Lowe and Murch *et al* (1999) Chapter 14.

relatively good allowance and did not have to become so involved with the child. A long-term foster carer had to make a bigger commitment to a child who perhaps had some special needs, yet the carer was less well rewarded financially.[28] In London High, the shortage of resources (financial and support) was generally felt to be a factor that may affect the outcome of a long-term plan and in more than one specific case the original care plan for adoption had had to be changed to a plan that embraced the possibilities of long-term fostering instead.

Residence order allowances[29]
Some authorities, like London Low, encouraged members of the extended family to apply to court to obtain a residence order rather than to be approved as long-term foster carers. However, one of the social workers felt that the allowances should then be made comparable with fostering allowances. It seemed ridiculous to her that a child should remain in care for want of a proper allowance and of proper support:

> *We've got to say that the children in need service is not just about child protection or a bit of family support for people with their own children; we ought to be looking at providing a "children in need family support service" for children who could be cared for under a residence order, so they're not stigmatised in the care system.*

In Metro High, on the other hand, there seemed to be some confusion about whether they made residence order allowances or not, although one

---

[28] It is to be noted that in Metro High the short-term foster rates were also much higher than the long-term foster rates.

[29] Under Sch 1, para 15 to the Children Act 1989 local authorities have a discretion to contribute to the cost of looking after a child who is living with a person in whose favour a residence order has been made. These allowances are known as residence order allowances. Payments of these allowances vary considerably, see for example, the *Residence Order Allowance Survey* conducted by the Grandparents' Federation (1996) and note also the Department of Health's *Residence Orders Study* conducted by the Social Services Inspectorate in 1995. It should be added that it is intended to introduce allowances for special guardians to be created by the Adoption and Children Bill. It seems likely that special guardianship will provide an alternative new option for relatives since it will provide for a more secure placement than a residence order but without severing the child's legal relationship from his or her birth family.

of the team leaders was under the impression that they were discretionary. One social worker said that there had been cases where relatives would have cared for a child if they had been given sufficient funds to support him or her financially. She believed this was preferable to the child being placed in a long-term fostering or adoptive placement. The ideal solution would appear to be to approve family members as carers (without necessarily being assessed as foster carers) and give them a generous allowance in line with the foster carers' allowance.

The extent to which budgetary constraints and the existence and rates of allowances for adopters, foster carers and residence orders have an influence on the execution of the plan is unclear. However, these appear to be the main effects:

- Long-term foster carers may be unable to accept the drop in income that appears to go with adoption.
- Extended family members may not be prepared to apply to court for a residence order because that may also mean a loss in income.
- Potential adopters may be lost because of the sudden drop in income, especially if they take on a child with special needs, although some authorities do offer additional allowances in such cases.

4.6 Extent of non-financial support offered to foster carers or adoptive families

Social workers in all our sample authorities thought that, alongside the financial support both for adopters and long-term foster carers, lack of social work support was an important factor in affecting the outcome of the plan.[30]

In Shire Low, all four social workers interviewed were concerned about the lack of support being offered, particularly post adoption. Post-adoption support appeared to last at best for a year, depending on the needs in each case, and thereafter depended on adoptive families referring themselves. Two social workers suggested that the lack of support might have two important consequences:

---

[30] Lack of social work support is also a factor in deterring family members from applying for a residence order.

(i) *Disrupted adoptions* One social worker was now working with several children where this had happened after they had been adopted for five or six years. In the past 'it was a case of, once they were adopted, over to you'. However, she thought that there was more post-adoption support nowadays.

(ii) *Loss of potential adopters* One social worker was convinced that potential adopters would be concerned about the lack of post-adoption support. As she put it :

There's the element of taking on board the responsibility – you've got the freedom to do that, but what support are you going to get if you need it? And how long is that support going to be?

She thought that the potential lack of support might also play a role in the social workers' choice of plan, not only in relation to adoption or long-term fostering, but also in their ability to encourage foster carers to seek residence orders.[31]

Another social worker in Shire Low expressed concern that people who had been trained and assessed as appropriate adopters had dropped out because of the lack of support while they were waiting for a child to be placed with them.

4.7   Availability of specialist services

None of the social workers in any of the authorities said that the availability or non-availability of specialist services needed for post-placement support would affect the choice of plan for the child.[32] However, in Shire Low, two social workers were concerned about the lack of child and adolescent mental health support which they considered essential to help children move on and cope with changes. They both said that, although

---

[31] The White Paper (ibid, paras 6.26–6.31) proposes that a more comprehensive and consistent post-adoption support package must be offered to adopters.

[32] Social workers in one of the London authorities which had access to all the necessary services thought that this would not in any way influence a plan being carried out but might affect the location of a placement.

the lack of such services would not affect the choice of plan, it might affect the possibility of success:

We do what we can in-house and keep our fingers crossed basically.

4.8   Other influences

Guardians ad litem

Several social workers representing all the sample authorities, mentioned the influence of guardians ad litem (now called children's guardians). Their views can be summed up as follows:

- Guardians are very powerful and influential with the court.
- Social workers' views are given less weight by the court.
- Social workers welcome the views of guardians as a fresh and independent eye on a case.
- Social workers try for the most part to work with the guardian because they are both seeking to secure what is best for the child.

In all authorities, social workers said that if the guardian disagreed with their plan for the child, they would not change it but would try to work in partnership to achieve some consensus. Only in the two London authorities did the social workers think that in some cases guardians had supported birth parents' interests rather than the child's. In Shire High, an authority which gave adoption a high profile, it was mentioned that guardians were increasingly opposing plans for adoption for older children and in other cases wanted to achieve a plan for the child which the Social Services Department could not realise because of lack of resources.[33]

Length of adoption proceedings

In Metro High, social workers expressed the view that the adoption process should be speeded up to make it more attractive to potential

---

[33] The creation of the Children and Family Courts Advisory and Support Service (CAFCASS) under the Criminal Justice and Courts Services Act 2000, which came into force in April 2001, presents, resources permitting, an opportunity to develop professional training in this capacity and to encourage effective cross-agency co-operation.

adopters.[34] They also pointed out that court timescales did not fit with children's timescales and that what may have been the best option at the start of the proceedings may not be by the end, especially considering that adopters are harder to find for older children.

Local authority legal departments

In one authority, two senior social workers expressed concern that their legal department appeared to be very cautious in its approach to the court and often tried to second-guess the magistrates, rather than allowing the social workers to take their cases to court to be heard and criticised, if necessary.

4.9 The Directors' views on adoption and long-term fostering

Perhaps reflecting different mixes of corporate philosophy, the availability of supply side resources (staff levels and skills, availability of foster carers, adopters, etc) and, of course, the local demand on the authorities' services, the Directors took differing views about when fostering might be more appropriate than adoption and vice versa. Nevertheless, confirming our interviews with their social workers, one clear message emerged above all others, namely, the importance of age as a determinant in the decision-making process, i.e. the younger the child the more appropriate adoption was thought to be. Related to this was the issue of contact with birth families which was more likely to arise in the case of older children where they thought fostering might be the more appropriate option.

Several Directors made the point that cultural, religious and financial factors can affect the acceptability of adoption. As one pointed out:

There is a whole range of circumstances where I think long-term fostering is just as good as adoption. You do not have to have adoption in order to guarantee stability. It's about stability – that's the key issue –

---

[34] Following the White Paper's proposal (ibid, at para 5.17) to introduce timescales in the adoption process, the Adoption and Children Bill makes provision for courts when hearing adoption proceedings to 'draw up a timetable with a view to determining such a question without delay'. This power is analagous to the courts' powers when determining Children Act 1989 proceedings.

consistency and stability. That's absolutely critical. Another factor is that adoption is something not understood by some ethnic minority groups.

He went on to explain that:

We've got situations where long-term fostering is perfectly stable, is the ideal arrangement because the birth parents still have contact. The idea of going through the whole legal process is anathema to everybody concerned. We've got many foster carers – I can think of one Muslim family who have got four placed children, who would never adopt. I would never want them to adopt because their total income for these four children is something like £1,200–£1,500 a week, because those children have all got special needs and it's much more appropriate that they provide a stable home and get that income. I would find it quite difficult to argue with even the most enlightened members of the council that adoptive parents should get a fee at that rate.

This last point of course raises yet again the issue of differential rates of allowances for adoption, fostering and residence orders.

5 Summary

5.1 Background

The following findings relate to 113 children, comprising 54 for whom adoption was the plan and 59 for whom long-term fostering was the plan. Of these 113:

- Only 87 (77%) had reasons for the plan recorded in the Care Plan or Statutory Review.
- Only 69 (61%) had *clear* reasons specifically relating to the plan for adoption (29 cases – 26%) or long-term fostering (40 cases – 35%).

5.2 Child-related factors affecting long-term plans

- *Age* seems the single most influential factor:
  - Children aged 1–4 years were twice as likely to be the subject of an adoption plan as for long-term fostering; conversely

- children aged 5–9 years were four times more likely to be the subject of a plan for long-term fostering as for adoption.
- No child aged 10–12 years was the subject of an adoption plan.
- Practice varied according to authority:
  - In Shire High all children aged 1–4 years were the subject of a plan for adoption but only 37% were in Shire Low; conversely
  - in Metro High, Metro Low and Shire Low all children aged 5–9 years were subject to a plan for long-term fostering but only 50% were in London High.
- Social workers generally thought the upper age limit for considering adoption was 9–11 years old, but some said 7–9.

Gender

Not specifically mentioned in case files nor by social workers when interviewed; but

- 57% of girls were the subject of an adoption plan as opposed to 41% of boys and for younger children the difference was more pronounced: viz. 80% of girls aged 1–4 years were subject to an adoption plan as against 53% of boys.

Ethnicity and culture

- Black and minority ethnic children were more likely to be the subject of a plan for long-term fostering than white children: 65% of minority ethnic children were the subject of a long-term fostering plan compared with 47% of white children.

Emotional and behavioural problems

- Children with emotional or behavioural problems or other special needs were more likely to be the subject of a long-term fostering plan (64%) than adoption (36%).

Evidence of abuse

- Children with no evidence of abuse were more likely to be the subject of an adoption plan (57%) than long-term fostering (43%) and were

marginally more likely to be so if there was evidence of neglect or emotional abuse – 51% adoption, 49% long-term fostering.
- Children who had been physically or sexually abused were more likely to be the subject of a long-term fostering plan (63%) than adoption (37%).

Child's wishes
- In 32% of cases the child's view had been taken into consideration, but in 43% of cases the child was said to be too young to express an opinion.
- In two cases adoption remained the plan despite the child's wishes to the contrary.

5.3   Family-related factors affecting long-term plans

- *Contact with birth family:* linked with age, the child's ongoing contact with the birth family seemed to be the most significant factor, i.e. the older the child the more significant the relationship with the birth family is likely to be and the greater the probability that long-term fostering would be the chosen plan.
  - The vast majority (85%) of children aged 5–9 years with ongoing direct contact with their birth mother were subject to a plan for long-term fostering as against 69% with either no or indirect contact; on the other hand:
  only 59% of children aged 1–4 years with ongoing direct contact with their birth mother were subject to a plan for long-term fostering as against 26% with either no or indirect contact.
  - This pattern varied by authority. For example, in Metro High 20% of children of all ages with ongoing direct contact with their birth mother were the subject of an adoption plan as against 44% of children in London Low.
  - Most children (75%) with ongoing direct contact with their birth father were the subject of a plan for long-term fostering.
  - Similarly, most children (67%) with ongoing direct contact with other family members were the subject of a plan for long-term fostering.

- Social workers considered it generally easier to recruit adopters for children who had little or no contact with their birth family.
- Most thought that in practice it was hard to make post-adoption contact work.

- *Extended family members as carers* were always said to be considered once rehabilitation to birth parents had been ruled out, but their availability did not necessarily affect choice of long-term plans; but
- Where a family member was assessed as suitable as a long-term carer, their status depended on the type and extent of the support they needed; they tended to be given foster carer status only where difficulties were anticipated.
- *Attachment to carers* was one of the most frequently cited reasons recorded in the case files for the child remaining with the current carer.
- *Sibling groups:* no clear picture emerged as to whether being part of a sibling group generally affected long-term planning, in part governed by the ages of children within sibling groups.
  - Despite preferences to keep siblings together it was not unusual for the younger sibling to be subject to a plan for adoption, with the older child being subject to a plan for long-term fostering.
  - Some authorities found it as hard to find a foster family for three or four siblings as to find an adoptive family.

5.4 Organisational-related factors affecting long-term plans

- *Local authority policies* varied in their extent of specifically advocating adoption. London High, for example, had a policy of planning for adoption regardless of the child's age and looked to long-term fostering as the "second best" alternative if no adoptive placement could be found. Shire High, on the other hand, did not particularly promote one long-term option over another.
- There was some evidence that individual team practice within authorities could affect the long-term planning decisions and thus be different from other team's decisions.
- *Availability both of adopters and foster carers* was generally acknowledged to be a difficulty and sometimes meant, particularly in the London authorities, that placement took precedence over cultural

concerns. However, we could not say that availability generally dictated what the long-term plan for the child should be.

- Nevertheless, the lack of available adopters could lead to delay in placing the child and occasionally to a change of plan, while the scarcity of long-term fostering placements could mean a child remaining in a holding placement for some time.

- Finding suitable and willing adopters for children with special needs, particularly those with severe emotional or behavioural problems or whose parents had a history of chronic mental health problems, was acknowledged to be a special difficulty.

- *Budgetary constraints* were sometimes mentioned as a consideration, but in Metro Low it was acknowledged to be an influential factor in decision-making as, for example, by not using foster carers from outside agencies because of their cost.

- *Adoption/long-term fostering allowances* were generally thought to be a factor as to why some short-term foster carers were unwilling to become long-term foster carers and long-term foster carers to become adopters since they would lose income.

- *Residence order allowances* seemed problematic, with not all social workers being sure that allowances were paid by their authority and a reported reluctance of extended family members (for whom this allowance is principally designed) being prepared to apply to court for a residence order in the first place.

- *Non-financial support* – a number of social workers thought that the lack of social work support, particularly but not exclusively post adoption, was an important factor affecting the outcome of a long-term plan.

- *The influence of guardians ad litem* was generally thought to be an important factor in determining the outcome of a long-term decision, particularly adoption. Social workers thought that the guardian's view carried more weight with the court than their view.

- *Length of adoption legal proceedings* was mentioned as a possible deterrent factor to would-be adopters.

References

The Grandparents' Federation (1996), *Residence Order Allowance Survey*, Harlow: Grandparents' Federation

Ivaldi G (2000), *Surveying Adoption: A comprehensive analysis of local authority adoptions 1998–1999*, London: BAAF

Lowe N and Murch M, Borkowski M, Weaver A, Beckford V with Thomas C (1999), *Supporting Adoption – Reframing the approach*, London: BAAF

Social Services Inspectorate (1995), *Residence Orders Study*, London: Department of Health

4 The length of the process

1 Introduction – the issue of detrimental delay

The second objective of this study was to collate information on the length of the decision-making process in relation to both adoption and long-term fostering, and in particular, to explore the issue of "delay". As already mentioned,[1] the term "delay" has to be qualified since it can be both purposeful as well as detrimental. As is observed in the research review *Adoption Now* (Parker, 1999, p. 21):

> *There is obviously a proper pace at which matters should proceed for the child, a pace that provides enough time for the necessary assessments to be made, agreements obtained and reports submitted . . . Placements can be made too hurriedly as well as too slowly.*

Gearing the pace to the needs of the child is vital. As we have written elsewhere (Lowe and Murch *et al*, 1999, p. 45):

> *All the professional thoroughness and care in the world can be nullified if the child's emotional resources are over-taxed and capacity to form a healthy attachment is damaged.*

A growing volume of studies and official reports testify that one of the hitherto intractable weaknesses of our current child care system and the slow-moving nature of court proceedings is that, following their removal from often dangerous and neglectful families, children can be placed in a series of short-term foster homes before permanent homes are found for them. Some who begin to form attachments in one foster home find they are then moved on, sometimes several times, before the authorities take the decision to find an adoptive or long-term foster home for them. Others can remain "in limbo" in care while awaiting the outcome of prolonged efforts to prepare for their eventual rehabilitation and return to their birth families. Yet often these efforts are unsuccessful. It is only then with

---

[1] See Chapter 1, para 1.

hindsight that it is appreciated that much time has been lost which could have been devoted to finding an alternative permanent home for the child.

Moreover, although children's resilience varies, it has to be remembered that particularly babies and infants have a different concept of time from that of adults and accordingly cannot tolerate uncertainty and delay in the same way as older children and adults. Parker's Research Review (1999, p. 121) concluded:

> There is a good deal of evidence in the studies about how delay – especially unexplained delay – causes uncertainty, anxiety and stress, both for children and prospective adopters.

A further often overlooked but vitally important point is that it is not enough simply to consider the issue of delay in the context of particular care episodes or categories of proceedings – the period from admission to permanency planning, adoption, care proceedings and the like. The risk of detrimental delay and drift, so often accompanied by a series of short-term placements, has to be considered in the context of the child's overall care history. The adverse effects on a child's behaviour, concentration levels, educational attainment and, above all, capacity to form secure attachments may well be cumulative. Schaffer (1993, p. 231), a leading developmental child psychologist, observes:

> Isolated crises need not lead to later disorder. Specific stresses are only of long-term significance if they are the first link in a chain of unfortunate events. Thus a child's removal from home may lead to a series of placements in unfavourable institutions and foster homes, each one adding to the child's insecurity and lack of identity and all helping eventually to bring about a disturbed personality ... It is the totality of experience as it impinges on the child throughout the formative years, rather than a specific event, that accounts for the end result. Not that this is any reason to take isolated stresses lightly! For one thing they produce suffering at the time and minimising that is plenty of justification for action; and for another, intervention at this point may prevent the formation of a chain of events that would otherwise follow on in an apparently relentless sequence.

2 Outline method of approach

Despite the different mechanics in the fostering and adoption decision-making processes, we needed to devise a yardstick which allowed us to compare the overall length of time taken for each option. To do this it was necessary to divide each process into a number of key stages which we have identified as follows:

Adoption and fostering

The point when:
- the child first became looked after;
- the plan for adoption or long-term fostering was formulated;
- the child was matched with potential adopters or long-term foster carers;
- the child was placed for adoption or in a long-term foster home;
- (adoption only) the adoption order was made.

2.1 Caveat

Certain limitations inherent in this approach need to be acknowledged. First, although the majority of the 113 cases in our Stage 3 sample drawn from the six local authorities followed the above sequence of events, not all did so. For example, the stage at which a child was placed with carers sometimes superseded the previous two stages, as the child may have been living with long-term foster carers or adopters before the plan for long-term fostering or adoption was made. This was most likely to happen when children were long-term fostered or adopted by relatives, or when short-term foster carers decided they would like to adopt the child or look after them on a long-term fostering basis. Such cases have therefore been excluded from certain parts of our analysis.

Secondly, it was not possible to provide a meaningful average time for the long-term fostering group between being "matched with carers" and being placed with them because so many of the children in the sample had been placed with carers before they were formally matched.

Thirdly, while our data collection tools were designed with the aim of charting the progress of a child subject to a long-term plan and while, in the majority of these cases, most of the stages were clearly identified, there was some doubt about the reliability of the data in certain instances. This was particularly so with respect to the precise date when the plan was formulated. The reason for this is that, as explained in Part I,[2] it was decided early in the project to record what the plan for a child was at 31 March 1999 and again at 31 March 2000. Consequently, although it was possible to identify when the child started to be looked after and the plan that was current at 31 March 1999, the data did not reveal whether there were any other long-term plans made between these dates which subsequently might have been abandoned. In some cases we were aware of such previous plans, but not all were recorded as we did not include this as a specific question on our data collection form.

Fourthly, a number of cases when sampled had not yet reached the later stages of our scheme, for example, being matched with long-term foster carers or adopters. This means that there are different totals for each stage, as will be seen in some of the tables below.[3]

Fifthly, the potential return to the birth family following attempts at rehabilitation is an important factor influencing the length of time a child is looked after by the local authority before plans for long-term fostering or adoption were made. For this reason, before we present our data concerning the length of the long-term fostering and adoption processes, we need to consider the data which we have collected concerning plans for rehabilitation.

3 Rehabilitation

It is possible that long periods of time, from the point that the child last became looked after until the date the plan for adoption or long-term fostering was made, can be explained in part by the existence of plans for rehabilitation to the birth family.

---

[2] See Chapter 1, pp. 17–18.

[3] The total number of cases was also affected by the fact that there was missing information at various points in the process.

3.1   Plans for rehabilitation

In 47 of the 113 case files (42%), there was evidence that there had been a plan for rehabilitation.[4] Of these, 26 (55%) later had a plan for adoption and 21 (45%) for long-term fostering. In only 14 of these 47 (30%) cases was the child ever placed at home.

3.2   Length of time between start of being looked after to plan for rehabilitation

Information on the length of time from the start of being looked after until the plan for rehabilitation was formed was available in relation to 33 of the 47 cases. In eight of these (24%), the plan was made at the time the child started to be looked after. In a further eight it was made within the first month. In 11 cases, the rehabilitation plan was made between the second month and the end of the first year. In a further six cases, rehabilitation plans were made after the first year.

The mean number of months between the start of being looked after and the formulation of a rehabilitation plan was four months for adoption cases and 11 months for long-term fostering cases.

3.3   Length of time of rehabilitation plan

Precise details of when the plan began and ended were only available in 27 out of the 47 cases where there was evidence of a plan for rehabilitation. The great majority of these ceased within 14 months but there were one or two cases where the rehabilitation plan continued for several years. Our evidence suggests that the mean average duration of the rehabilitation plan in the case of the adoption group was 16 months and, in the long-term fostering group, two years.

---

[4] In another 53 case files (47%), it was recorded that there was no evidence of a previous plan for rehabilitation. In a further nine files rehabilitation was recorded as inapplicable since the child was accommodated. In four files it was not apparent whether there had been a plan for rehabilitation or not.

3.4   Length of time rehabilitation attempted

Only one authority, Shire Low, appeared to have a clear policy about monitoring attempts at rehabilitation in order to avoid drift. Here by the time of the third review, after six or seven months, if the child had not returned home to the birth family the case had to be considered by a special children's panel. Elsewhere in the five other authorities, social workers told us that there were no specific procedures regulating how long rehabilitation should be attempted.

We were told that in London Low the decision on whether to end attempts at rehabilitation was generally taken at statutory reviews. Even so, social workers thought there could still be a danger of drift because some social workers have difficulty in making tough decisions in their work with birth parents and because the Children Act 1989, in any event, reinforced this approach. In addition, one social worker suggested to us that the recent implementation of the Human Rights Act 1998 and, in particular, its incorporation into domestic law of Article 8 of the European Convention on Human Rights (i.e. the right to respect for private and family life), could encourage birth parents to challenge the local authority's plans for adoption.[5]

In Shire High and in both metropolitan authorities, although there were no specific guidelines on how long rehabilitation should be attempted, timetables were said to be often built into individual care plans. It was then left to the social worker's discretion to manage the case in the light of these targets according to the child's age and needs.

---

[5] The soundness of this view is debatable, for while it is certainly true that *parents'* rights are protected by Article 8, it is well established both by European Court of Human Rights' decisions and domestic law that under the Convention, where there is 'serious conflict between the interests of a child and one of its parents which could only be resolved to the disadvantage of one of them, the interests of the child had to prevail . . .', per Butler-Sloss P in *Re L (Contact: Domestic Violence)*; *Re V (Contact: Domestic Violence)*; *Re M (Contact: Domestic Violence)*; *Re H (Contact: Domestic Violence)* [2001] Fam 260 at 277, [2000] 2 FLR 334 at 346 relying inter alia upon *Johansen v Norway* (1996) 23 EHRR 33 at 72 and *Hendriks v Netherlands* (1982) 5 EHRR 223. See also Thorpe L J in *Payne v Payne* [2001] EWCA Civ 166, [2001] 1 FLR 1051, CA.

3.5 Reasons for abandoning rehabilitation plans (from the Stage 3 data)

Social workers suggested various factors which could affect their decision on whether to abandon a plan for rehabilitation. These included whether the child was at significant risk of harm; whether the birth parents demonstrated an unwillingness to work with the authority and address the issues which had led to the child being looked after in the first place; and a range of other deep-rooted problems which were unlikely to be resolved within a reasonable time, taking account of the child's age.

The following list, based on 37 cases in which the plan appeared subsequently to have been abandoned, gives the range of primary reasons as stated on the file:[6]

- Birth mother could not cope with the behaviour of or meet the needs of the child (N = 9).
- Parents/parent had been assessed as unsuitable (N = 8).
- Instances of sexual abuse or family violence (N = 6).
- Birth parents unco-operative with social services department (N = 6).
- Home environment too unstable (N = 4).
- Serious mental illness of birth mother (N = 4).

---

[6] In other cases the reason for terminating the rehabilitation plan could not be found in the file.

4 Comparison of the length of the process for adoption and long-term fostering

Table 23
Time before long-term plan formulated and child matched

| Key stage | Average time (Number of cases) | | | |
| | Adoption | | Long-term fostering | |
	Duration	No:	Duration	No:
Start to be looked after → plan	1 year 3 mths	(54)	2 years 4 mths	(59)
Plan formulated → matching with carers	9 mths	(31)	4 mths	(32)
Start to be looked after → placement with carers	1 year 11 mths	(39)	1 year 7 mths	(41)

Table 23 shows the average time children in the sample had been looked after by the authority before a plan for adoption or long-term fostering was made and the average time spent from the plan being formulated until adopters or long-term foster carers were identified. The average used is the arithmetic mean.

The first point to note is how plans for long-term fostering took on average more than a year longer to be formulated than those for adoption. We are not sure why this should be so. It could be that the long-term fostering sample, being on average an older age group, contained more children where the local authority was attempting rehabilitation with their own families, though from the information we have, [7] this is only likely to be of marginal importance. Another possible reason is that this group might have had more previous plans (for example, adoption) which were later abandoned during this period in favour of the long-term fostering option.

Secondly, it took on average more than twice as long to match children with adopters after the plan was formulated than it did to match children with long-term foster carers. Again, we can only speculate as to the reasons. It may be that for some of the children the identity of the

---

[7] See above, para 3.1.

long-term foster carers was known at the time the plan for long-term fostering was made, thus reducing the average time spent during this stage of the process. Alternatively, it may be that authorities would be more meticulous in placing children for adoption possibly mindful that they would have to account for their decision to a court.

5 Adoption: the length of the process

Table 24
Timing of key stages in the adoption process

Key stage in adoption process	Average time (mean)	Number of cases
Start to be looked after → Plan	1 year 3 months	54
Plan formulated → Matching	9 months	31*
Matching → Placed for adoption	1 month	29*
Placed for adoption → Adoption order	1 year 2 months	15
Plan formulated → Adoption order	1 year 11 months	15
Start to be looked after → Adoption order	3 years 1 month	15

*Although, as will be seen from **Table 23** above, we have data concerning 39 cases which cover the period from when the child started to be looked after until being placed with carers, missing data in the case files concerning the intervening periods account for the lower totals appearing in this Table.

Table 24 above shows the average duration, based on the arithmetic mean, of each consecutive key stage in the adoption process. It also shows the average time spent between a plan for adoption being formulated and an adoption order being made and the overall average time spent looked after until an adoption order is made. The two stages in the adoption process, which, on average, took the longest, were first, between starting to be looked after and the plan being formulated; and second, between being placed for adoption and the adoption order being made.

In interpreting **Table 24** above, the first thing to note is that the size of the sample reduces at each stage of the process. This is because the sample drawn was based on children where there was a *plan* for adoption, not, as in other studies, where adoption orders had been made. In other words, we were looking at children at various stages in the pipeline. It is to be particularly noted that of the 54 children in our sample for whom adoption was the plan, only 15 had so far been adopted.

5.1   Cardiff data compared with other findings

Some of the above timescales can be compared with other published statistics on lengths of the various stages of the adoption process. It must be remembered, however, that although our data compare closely, the national findings to which we refer here were based on children of all ages who were being looked after, whereas our sample did not include children who were over 13 years old or under one year old on 31 March 1999. However, this does not appear to have made much, if any, difference in the general comparisons.

The Department of Health's White Paper, *Adoption: A new approach* (para 2.8) considered that decisions about adoption are not made early enough and that when plans for adoption are made they are delivered too slowly. The findings of Ivaldi (2000, pp. 54–80) and Department of Health statistics[8] are used to illustrate these points. Our findings on the length of the adoption process are very similar. Thus, as can be seen from **Table 24** above, we found that the average time a child spent being looked after until a plan for adoption was formulated for a child was one year three months. This very closely matches the findings of Ivaldi (2000). He found that children waited an average of one year four months after becoming looked after before a plan for adoption was formulated (p. 58).

Our findings on the length of time spent between the decision for adoption being made and being placed for adoption also match closely Ivaldi's study. Our findings show an average time of 10 months. Ivaldi found an average time of five months for babies who were under one month old when they started to be looked after, but 11 months for children over five, and seven months for all children adopted (2000, p. 57).

The Department of Health's statistics show an average overall period of nearly three years from when children start to be looked after until they are adopted.[9] We found that the children in our sample waited on average three years one month.

---

[8] See para 2.8 of the Adoption White Paper.
[9] Adoption White Paper at p. 15.

We also compared our findings on the length of the adoption process with the findings of the BAAF survey 1998/9 (Ivaldi, 1999). The similarities of the findings are displayed in **Table 25** below.

Table 25
Average timescales for looked after children adopted: our sample compared to the BAAF survey 1998/9 (all ages) (mean)

	Plan → *matching*	*Matching →* *placement*	*Placed →* *adoption*	*Plan →* *adoption*
BAAF data	6 months	1 month	1 year 2 months	1 year 9 months
Cardiff data	9 months	1 month	1 year 2 months	1 year 11 months

5.2   Cardiff data compared with LAC (98) 20 targets

The LAC (98) 20 set targets within which particular stages of the adoption process should be reached. Different targets were set, depending on whether the child was a baby or an older child at the point of first starting to become looked after. Data were collected on 952 children for whom adoption was the plan from 34 social services departments and the results were compared with the targets. As there were only seven children in our sample who were less than a month old at the time they started to be looked after, we have not attempted to compare the data on these children with the LAC (98) 20 targets for babies.

The targets for older children were as follows: plan to be made within nine months of being looked after; to panel within two months later; matched with an adoptive family within six months of the panel recommendation and placed for adoption within two months of matching.

In **Table 26** below we compare our data comprising 47 older children for whom adoption was the plan at 31 March 1999 with the LAC (98) 20 (para 2.8) targets and results. It should be noted that none of the children in our sample were aged over 13 at 31 March 1999; consequently the average age of the children in our sample will be lower than that used for the LAC (98) 20 targets.

Table 26
Comparison of our data with those used for the LAC (98) 20 targets for older children

Stages	LAC data	Cardiff data
Started to be looked after → plan (target 9 months)[10]	65%	36%
Matching → placement[11] (target 2 months)	88%	92%
Started to be looked after → adoption[12] (target 18 months)	–	9%

The startling finding contained in **Table 26** is that only 36 per cent of our sample of older children met the target of nine months for the key initial period between starting to be looked after and a plan being formulated. The unanswered question is why it took so long in our sample for the majority to reach this stage. The possible impact of rehabilitation plans may be a cause. However, once a match with prospective adopters had been made, the large majority of the 25 cases reaching this point were placed within two months (92%). A second startling point is that very few (9%) of the 11 older children in our sample were adopted within the target of 18 months. This finding confirms the point made in the White Paper (para 2.8) that:

Permanent placements, including adoption ... are not delivered quickly enough, from the point of view of the child's timescales.

Indeed our data concerning the overall length of the adoption process match those reported in the Department of Health Statistics (para 2.8), namely that:

Children wait on average nearly three years from becoming continuously looked after to being adopted.

---

[10] Data were only available on 47 older children.
[11] Data were only available on 25 older children.
[12] This analysis is based on the 11 older children who had been adopted by 31 March 2000.

As can be seen from **Table 26,** a higher percentage of the cases in our sample met the target time between matching and placement for adoption compared to the LAC results, but a significantly lower percentage met the target time between starting to be looked after and the plan being formulated. Only nine per cent of our sample were within the target set for the overall time of being looked after before being adopted. There was no comparable figure in the LAC results.

6 The problem of multiple placements

As already mentioned,[13] the issue of delay is associated with the problem of multiple placements. Mindful of this we decided, when examining the 113 case files in Stage 3, to collect what information we could about the number of placements that the children had apparently experienced. What emerged was that there was a substantial minority – about a third – who experienced four or more placements and 14 children who had six or more. Before examining these data more closely we should emphasise the following.

First, it is easy in considering statistical data of this kind to forget the many acute human dramas and tragedies which they represent. Researchers and policy makers have to beware of the dangers of a defensive flight into objectivity. Each episode of arriving in a new home implies leaving a previous one. Child placement, whether in a foster or adoptive home following separation from the birth family, is likely to tax the emotional resources of any child, however sensitively the process is managed by social workers and the child's new carers. A study by Thomas and Beckford (1999) of children's accounts of adoption reports that the 'majority only recall varying degrees of shyness and fear' about meeting their prospective adopters for the first time and that 'with few exceptions the children did not feel included in the preparation and presentation of information about themselves for their new families'. Moves from one home to another meant, as Thomas and Beckford put it (p. 64):

---

[13] See para 1 above.

. . . significant changes in almost every aspect of the children's lives – a new family home, neighbourhood, school and friends. They had to cope with new relationships and a strange environment and make many adjustments. The early days of their new placements were often experienced as puzzling and stressful.

One can only add that the greater the number of moves, the greater the likelihood of repeated stress and system-induced harm resulting from cumulative damage to the child (see Schaffer, 1993).

Secondly, when considering our statistical data, it should be noted that, if anything, they are likely to under-represent the true incidence of the numbers of moves which the children will have experienced. This is partly because for many, the placement process was incomplete at the point when the files were sampled. Furthermore, because we collected data concerning only the present period of being looked after, our analysis does not take account of any additional placements children may have experienced in previous periods of being looked after. Ivaldi's (2000) study of adoption shows that 29 per cent of the BAAF sample of 1,801 adopted children had experienced four or more placements (p. 29). That figure rises to a startling 44 per cent in the case of infants when entering care aged 1–12 months. In another study of 249 children looked after for between 12 and 24 months in six local authorities, Skuse and Ward (2000) found that 28 per cent had experienced three or more placements and 16 per cent, four or more.[14] Although the social workers responsible for these children classified 54 per cent of the changes of placement as "planned transitions" and although relatively few occurred because of disruptions, Skuse and Ward comment:

These findings reinforce concerns that the care system itself may create a sense of unpredictability which obstructs the development of attachment in very young children.

---

[14] This brief research report also mentions that a team from Loughborough University is currently conducting a study of 50 social workers about their use of "planned transitions" in an attempt to establish a clearer understanding of what they mean by this term.

6.1   Findings[15]

Table 27
The number of placements by plan

Number of placements	Adoption		Long-term fostering		Total	
	No:	%	No:	%	No:	%
1	5	(9%)	13	(23%)	18	(16%)
2	18	(34%)	21	(36%)	39	(35%)
3	11	(20%)	6	(10%)	17	(15%)
1–3	34	(63%)	40	(69%)	74	(66%)
4–5	16	(29%)	9	(16%)	25	(23%)
6–10	4	(8%)	9	(15%)	13	(12%)
Total	54		58		112	

Table 27 above shows that 31 per cent of the long-term fostering group and 37 per cent of the adoption group had experienced four or more placements. In other words, notwithstanding that they are younger on average, there is a tendency for children for whom adoption is planned, to have experienced more moves than those for whom long-term fostering is planned.

As can be seen from **Table 28** below, when the number of placements are correlated by the local authority it is clear that they vary widely. London High had the highest incidence of placements per child – with 10 children (54%) experiencing four or more – while Shire Low had the lowest incidence, with three children (21%) having four or more placements.

Another way of examining this variation is to compare the average number of placements per authority. **Table 29** below sets these out in rank order, again revealing the contrast between London High and Shire Low.

---

[15] Note: The following analysis is based on 112 cases rather than 113 as there was missing information on one case at each stage of the analysis. Furthermore, the percentages in the following tables do not always add up to an exact 100 per cent as they have been rounded to the nearest whole number.

Table 28
The number of placements by local authority

Number of placements	Number of cases within local authority						
	London High	London Low	Metro High	Metro Low	Shire High	Shire Low	Total
	No: %	No: %	No: %	No: %	No: %	No: %	No: %
1	1 (5%)	3 (16%)	4 (20%)	3 (15%)	3 (15%)	4 (27%)	1 (16%)
2	5 (26%)	6 (32%)	9 (45%)	7 (35%)	8 (40%)	4 (29%)	3 (35%)
3	3 (16%)	3 (16%)	1 (5%)	6 (30%)	1 (5%)	3 (21%)	1 (15%)
1–3	9 (47%)	12 (64%)	14 (70%)	16 (80%)	12 (60%)	11 (77%)	1 (66%)
4–5	5 (27%)	5 (27%)	6 (30%)	2 (10%)	4 (20%)	3 (21%)	2 (23%)
6–10	5 (27%)	2 (10%)	– –	2 (10%)	4 (20%)	– –	1 (12%)

Table 29
Average number of placements by local authority

Local authority	Average number of placements	Number of cases
London High	4.1	19
Shire High	3.6	20
London Low	3.1	19
Metro Low	2.8	20
Metro High	2.7	20
Shire Low	2.5	14

Table 30 below breaks down this analysis according to whether the plan was adoption or long-term fostering. It can be seen that, on average, the adoption group experienced slightly more placements, 3.2 compared with 3.1, than the long-term fostering group, but that in four authorities the position is reversed.

Table 30
Number of placements by local authority and plan

Local authority	Plan	Average number of placements	Number of cases
London High	Adoption	4.0	10
	Long-term fostering	4.2	9
	Total	4.1	19
London Low	Adoption	2.8	10
	Long-term fostering	3.4	9
	Total	3.1	19
Metro High	Adoption	3.4	10
	Long-term fostering	1.9	10
	Total	2.7	20
Metro Low	Adoption	2.5	10
	Long-term fostering	3.0	10
	Total	2.8	20
Shire High	Adoption	3.0	10
	Long-term fostering	4.2	10
	Total	3.6	20
Shire Low	Adoption	4.3	4
	Long-term fostering	1.8	10
	Total	2.5	14
Total	Adoption	3.2	54
	Long-term fostering	3.1	58
	Total	3.1	112

Table 31 below sets out an analysis of data concerning the number of placements according to the age when the child started to be looked after. On the face of it, overall, the average number of placements does not differ between the 1–4 and the 5–9 age groups. Closer analysis, however, reveals wide variations between authorities. For example, whereas in London High children aged between one and four years experienced an average of five placements, in Metro Low they experienced an average of only 2.6 placements.

Table 31
Number of placements by local authority and age

Local authority	Age at start of being looked after	Average number of placements	Number of cases
London High	1–4	5.0	11
	5–9	3.0	8
	10+	–	–
	Total	4.1	19
London Low	1–4	3.0	12
	5–9	3.3	7
	10+	–	–
	Total	3.1	19
Metro High	1–4	3.0	13
	5–9	2.0	6
	10+	2.0	1
	Total	2.7	20
Metro Low	1–4	2.6	15
	5–9	3.0	5
	10+	–	–
	Total	2.8	20
Shire High	1–4	3.1	8
	5–9	4.3	10
	10+	2.0	2
	Total	3.7	20
Shire Low	1–4	2.7	11
	5–9	2.0	3
	10+	–	–
	Total	2.5	14
Total	1–4	3.2	70
	5–9	3.2	39
	10+	2.0	3
	Total	3.1	112

6.2   Concluding comment

Even allowing for the comparatively small size of our sample and for the fact that our study was restricted to just six local authorities, these data, together with other studies such as the recent BAAF adoption data,[16] suggest to us that there is a need for further research to examine variations in the incidence of multiple placements between authorities, to explore their causes, and to investigate their consequences for and impact upon the children concerned. This is necessary not only in relation to adopted children but also to those who are fostered long-term or who end up in residential care.

7 Summary

7.1   Rehabilitation

- Of the 113 cases, there was evidence on the case files that a plan for rehabilitation had been made for 47 of them (42%).
- Of these 47 cases, 26 (55%) later had a plan for adoption and 21 (45%) for long-term fostering.
- The mean number of months between the start of being looked after and the formulation of the plan for rehabilitation was four months for adoption cases and 11 months for long-term fostering cases.
- The average duration of rehabilitation plans was 16 months for adoption cases and two years for long-term fostering cases.
- Only Shire Low had a specific policy or procedure concerning the length of time rehabilitation should be attempted.
- The most commonly expressed reasons, either as recorded in the children's case files or stated by social workers for terminating rehabilitation, were:
  - i)   parents being unable to cope with or meet the needs of the child;
  - ii) parents being assessed as unsuitable;
  - iii) instances of sexual abuse and family violence;
  - iv) parents unwilling to co-operate with social services.

---

[16] See Ivaldi (2000). We understand this is also a subject which Professor Sonia Jackson of Swansea University is investigating.

7.2 Comparison of the length of the process of adoption and long-term fostering

- Plans for long-term fostering took, on average, more than a year longer to be formulated than plans for adoption.
- It took, on average, twice as long for children to be matched with adopters as with long-term foster carers.

7.3 The length of the adoption process

- The average time from starting to be looked after to an adoption order was three years and one month.
- It took on average one year and three months from when the child first started to be looked after to the point when the plan for adoption was made.
- On average it took a further nine months from formulating the plan to match with prospective adopters and on average a further month before the child was placed.
- These data are similar to the findings reported in the Department of Health's Adoption White Paper.

7.4 The problem of multiple placements

Based on our analysis of the sample of 113 children:

- 31% of the long-term fostering group and 37% of the adoption group had experienced four or more placements.
- The incidence of multiple placements differs substantially between authorities, ranging from 21% with four or more placements in Shire Low to 54% in London High.
- There was a similarly wide variation between local authorities in the overall average number of placements, ranging from 2.5 in Shire Low to 4.1 in London High.
- On average the adoption group experienced slightly more placements than the long-term fostering group, 3.2 compared with 3.1.
- Local authorities differed widely when the number of placements is correlated by the age of the child, for example, the children in the 1–4

year age group experienced an average of five placements in London High but only 2.6 placements in Metro Low.

References

Ivaldi G (1999), *BAAF Adoption Survey 1998/99: Report on the preparatory phase*, London: BAAF

Ivaldi G (2000), *Surveying Adoption: A comprehensive analysis of local authority adoptions 1998–1999*, London: BAAF

Lowe N and Murch M, Borkowski M, Weaver A, Beckford V with Thomas C (1999), *Supporting Adoption – Reframing the approach*, London: BAAF

Parker R (ed) (1999), *Adoption Now: Messages from research*, London: Department of Health

Schaffer H R (1993), *Making Decisions about Children: Psychological questions and answers*, Oxford: Blackwell

Skuse T and Ward H (2000), *Looking After Children: Transforming data into management information*, London: Department of Health

Thomas C and Beckford V with Lowe N and Murch M (1999), *Adopted Children Speaking*, London: BAAF

5   Additional findings

1 Local authority responses to the Quality Protects Programme and to the individual inspections

The introduction of the Quality Protects Programme[1] has helped at least four of the local authorities to support their adoption function and has enabled them to monitor their performance in a more systematic way. It has provided a big impetus for them to improve their system which, before Quality Protects was initiated, was lacking in resources and focus.[2]

As well as taking on board the Quality Protects Programme, two local authorities had been the subject of recent SSI inspections. It was reported to us that, as a result of these inspections, both had been forced to examine their procedures and practices. Both authorities were encouraged to take on a more corporate responsibility for child care (for example, involving councillors, professionals from health, education and housing, foster carers and young people to serve on the Corporate Parent Committee). This had resulted in a more integrated service.

1.1   Directors' reactions to the Quality Protects initiative

The upside

The Directors were asked how they viewed the Government's Quality Protects initiative. All felt that it was valuable and had provided a much needed spur to action. A typical comment was:

> *I welcome it hugely. I welcome the focused attention from Government on children's personal and social services. I welcome the additional funds. I think it's very refreshing to have a Government which is committed to putting resources into and caring about children's social*

---

[1] Viz. that outlined in LAC 98(20).
[2] Early evidence shows that the programme is beginning to deliver improved outcomes for looked after children in terms of reducing the number of placement moves and increasing the number of children being adopted.

services. It feels as though the Government is still very critical of social services, but it is standing alongside rather than trying to jump up and down on top of us.

And the Director of the London authority, which was taking a number of new initiatives following an adverse SSI report, said:

It has been a Godsend to me. It meant that we have got some develop-ment monies at a time when particularly children's budgets have been very difficult. It's helped us achieve a whole range of things here. Cer-tainly it has helped us refocus our childcare work around education. It has opened up children's access to elected members. It has allowed us to do a lot of things like the Drop-In Centre for accommodated children and to ensure that young people are listened to in a much more constructive way. I would say that it has been overwhelmingly positive in terms of supporting family placements in being able to put a lot of money into that area too.

Another Director made the point that some of the mandatory requirements of the Quality Protects initiative, such as the need to complete Manage-ment Action Plans, enabled her to cut through a staff culture of having lengthy discussions before doing anything. As she said:

It's been good. It's been hard work but it's been a help in some ways not having a choice about what you are doing. Because you can tell the staff: 'I'm sorry, I know it's a lot of work but we have just got to get on with it.' That's better than the more usual: 'Let's have a working agree-ment to think about the possible best ways we might be able to improve practice,' which takes so much longer.

Yet another made the point that the requirements of the Quality Protects initiative complemented the Government's social inclusion policy agenda by firmly encouraging social services departments to collaborate more closely with educational and health authorities in the service of accom-modated children. In one authority, this has given rise to a powerful co-ordinating mechanism known as the Corporate Parenting Panel. Here, the elected members, who chair various authority committees, together with the Directors of social services, housing and education departments, meet with representatives of looked after young children under the overall chairmanship of the Chief Executive to consider local childcare policy initiatives. We were told that such initiatives help to break down an attitude of mind which tends to see social services as something of a professional ghetto that has to deal with all the intractable social problems that beset children in care.

In another authority, the Director specifically welcomed the way the Quality Protects initiative had forced her colleagues to give greater attention to the health care of looked after children. She told us:

> *Without it, health would not have been given enough priority. We find that when children come to our secure unit from all over the country – children who may have had between 10–15 placements – we find that they often have major health problems or poor eyesight or hearing problems that have never been properly investigated or treated.*

The downside
Despite such favourable comments about the Quality Protects initiative, there were also a number of reservations.

First, several Directors reported that it had resulted in an expansion of specialist posts which had siphoned off some good fieldwork staff who had been difficult to replace. As one of the Metropolitan Directors told us:

> *Since the advent of Quality Protects and the consequent increase in child care social work posts, there is a national recruitment problem and we are finding that there are just not enough qualified social workers. We are increasingly getting people straight from training courses and having to put them straight into front-line posts because the more experienced staff move into the more interesting and exciting Quality Protects developments. The result is a less experienced front-line child care staff than we had two or three years ago.*

Another criticism was that it had not dealt with some of the most fundamental problems confronting local authority childcare services, perhaps because it was considered a one-off initiative. As one of the Directors put it:

It has failed to address some of our most basic problems: wherever you look residential care is falling apart; while with respect to family placements – although we were able to put a lot of money into it – the fundamental issue is about whether we should shift to a professionalised foster or family placement service with elements of reward built into it. To do that you are talking about really big money on a long-term basis.

One of the Metropolitan Borough Directors endorsed this comment, saying:

The most worrying thing for me as a Director is the uncertainty of not knowing whether the money is going to be recurrent or non-recurrent. That has been a big worry for Directors because to try and really plan improvements in childcare services is a very difficult thing to do just on a three-year basis. You do not know whether you are going to have the money for the post near the end of this period. We have had to assume that the money will continue because you can't set up review teams and not have them continue. You can't expand after-care services that desperately need expansion given our growing number of looked after children and not have the current investment continue.

2 Policy problems

2.1 Variation of written policies

First, we need to clarify our use of the term "written policy". By policy we mean a clearly stated and explained strategic approach to the long-term planning for children being looked after by local authorities, grounded in research-based evidence and childcare theories. This is necessary so that it can be clearly understood both *why* the policy is what it is and the procedural steps and guidelines which flow from it. In fact we have found that practitioners, both social workers and Directors of Social Services, often do not make clear distinctions between written policies, unwritten policies, procedures and guidelines. All tend to be lumped together as "policies". What was referred to as written policy in discussions often appeared to be guidelines on procedure and practice, or what might be considered a "policy-in-action document".

We found little evidence of any written policy (as we define it) in any of the authorities investigated, save one – Shire Low. This authority had policies covering all aspects of child care. It had evidently been inspected recently and was criticised for having a low adoption rate. In another local authority (Shire High), comprehensive guidelines on both adoption and, more generally, on services for children in need had been reviewed and updated following the Quality Protects Programme. At the other extreme, one authority was said to be (by the authority's operation manager) 'under policied' and still using a 'very old procedural manual' dating from the early 1990s (post Children Act). At least two authorities had no written policy or guidelines on fostering or adoption. The social workers we talked to in Metro Low (where there was a general absence of written policies) felt that general policy, procedures and guidelines on permanence were of no help in the decision-making process when planning for long-term care.

Directors were asked whether their authorities had written policies to guide the adoption/long-term fostering decision-making process. Our impression was that preparation of written policy is largely delegated by Directors. Nevertheless their replies were illuminating and contrasting. For example, one of the Shire Directors referred to a very extensive policy document known locally as 'The White Book'. He referred to this as 'the Bible' telling us:

> *This tries to ground adoption policy and practice within a more general framework of policy and practice guidance for dealing with all looked after children in the authority.*

This department was in the process of updating it in order to make it compliant with national standards.

By contrast, the Director of one of the Metropolitan authorities, when asked whether there was a written policy, replied:

> *In terms of who should be considered for adoption, etc, I think not. We are just in the middle of an adoption review and that is one of the issues that has been identified as an area where we need to have an actual*

policy statement. So as yet we have no policy statement on adoption and none on long-term fostering as such either.

When asked whether there was any written policy about permanence, we were told:

I might be wrong and I would need to check this out, but I am not sure that there is anything actually written, but there are strong unwritten policies that are put through reviews, etc. There are some general statements on our child care policy which covers things like planning, the importance of children not drifting, that family placement (i.e. with parents or relatives) would be a placement of choice, but it doesn't go into details about when you'd consider adoption and when you'd consider long-term fostering.

2.2   Variation in subject areas covered by policy (written or oral)

Rehabilitation

The social workers we interviewed often referred to "policies" on specific areas of child care. For example, Shire Low had a written policy which clearly stated that they would not accommodate any child until all community support and extended family members had been tried. Although Shire Low was the only one of our sample authorities to have their policy on rehabilitation clearly documented, a similar policy was apparently frequently followed in the other authorities. We were told by social workers in these authorities that rehabilitation is the first option to consider when assessing the needs of a looked after child (which is in line with the general principles of the Children Act 1989). Shire High, for example, had recently established a strategy requiring rehabilitation to be part of their positive planning policy. This meant that an important question at each review, while the child is being looked after, was whether he or she should remain in care or accommodation or return home. Social workers in London High also felt that rehabilitation was their strong point – 'our job is to try to keep families together and not to break them up'. In London Low, however, where rehabilitation was always tried first, there was a feeling that this can lead to problems if it is carried out for too long to the detriment of the child who might shuttle in and out of care.

Timescales

Only one authority, Shire Low, had introduced mechanisms in order to try to avoid drift.[3] For example, as we have already mentioned,[4] if, by the third review, a child had not been rehabilitated, the case had to go to a special children's panel and as one social worker put it 'the heat is on' to make and implement a long-term plan. In Shire High a system of triggers had been established so that cases which were not moving forward within a specified time, could be identified by the Area Manager who would ensure that progress was made. Nevertheless, we were told that in the main it appears that each case is judged according to the circumstances and that the pace of the process is left to the discretion of the social workers. However, in cases where there are court proceedings, the court may lay down timescales for attempts at rehabilitation.

Placement with extended family

Most authorities had "policies" concerning placement with the extended family if rehabilitation with birth parents was no longer an option. However, this policy became somewhat vague when the status of these carers was considered. In some authorities family members were auto-matically assessed as foster carers for the child, thus qualifying them for a foster carer's allowance. In other areas they were encouraged to apply for a residence order. Social workers from a couple of authorities thought that, if at all possible, it would be better for family members to be given the status of a foster carer with parental responsibility because of the

---

[3] Following the proposal in the Adoption White Paper, op cit at Ch 4, timescales are to be laid down within which decisions for most children should be reached and action taken. The overall target (see LAC (2001) 33) is that by 31 March 2005, at least 95 per cent of looked after children should be placed for adoption within 12 months of the decision that adoption is in the child's best interests (up from 81% in 2001). More specific timescales are set in *National Adoption Standards for England*, op cit at A2 and A3, namely, the child's need for a permanent home will be addressed at the four month review and where adoption is identified as the plan at that review the adoption panel will make its recommendation within two months. In care proceedings, where adoption is the plan a match with suitable adoptive parents will be identified and approved by a panel within six months of the court's decision (three months where a panel has requested a child aged under six months to be placed for adoption).

[4] See Chapter 4, para 3.4.

perceived stigma of looking after a child under the care of social services.

Linked to the issue of the status of extended family carers is the question of financial support. Generally speaking, the amount of a foster carer's allowance is greater than that received by a carer who has been granted a residence order.[5] In London Low we were told that residence order allowances were means-tested. Furthermore, once a residence order is granted, parental responsibility shifts to the carer and the social services department is then no longer *required* to offer support. These factors tended to make a residence order an unattractive option for relatives. Some local authorities were trying to address this problem by supporting members of the extended family in different ways. For example, in Shire Low placements with family members were classified as a "friends and relatives placement" and given a generous package on a par with foster carers. Furthermore, for those relatives granted a residence order, social services offered a "Letter of Commitment" detailing support. Similarly, in Shire High there was a "Friends and Family Placement Scheme" offering financial support. A social worker from London High thought that the best way of addressing this problem would be to approve the family members as carers for that specific child (without necessarily being assessed as foster carers) but at the same time recommending them for a generous allowance in line with that paid to foster carers.

Adoption by foster carers

Policy also seemed to vary between authorities on the issue of whether foster carers should be able to adopt. In 46 cases where suitable adopters had been identified, 13 children had been previously fostered by their adopters (28%). Overall, there was a very slight difference according to whether the authority was classed as a "high" or "low" user of adoption. The "high" users tended not to use foster carers as adopters, with 21 out of 27 of their cases being in this group (78%), whereas the "low" users of adoption had 63 per cent of their cases in this group. Indeed, in Shire Low this type of adoption was actively discouraged by the local authority.[6] In

---

[5] See Chapter 3, paras 3.2 and 4.5 (at pp. 74–76).
[6] For further discussion of local authority attitudes to adoption by foster carers, see Lowe and Murch *et al* (1999 pp. 96–97).

both Metro High and London High the social workers thought that historically the department was reluctant to use foster carers as adopters as it was seen as losing a potential resource. However, in both these areas the policy appeared to be changing. Social workers in Shire High thought that foster carers who wished to adopt would be advised to consider residence orders instead. On the other hand, in London Low, we were told that foster carers would be encouraged to apply for adoption if they wanted to do so or for residence orders because it was 'good for carers and children to see that the decision-makers in their lives are the people looking after them and not some fairly random person sitting in an area office'. In Metro Low there appeared to be no underlying policy on permitting foster carers to adopt and it seemed to occur on an ad hoc basis.[7]

Use of freeing orders

We found a wide variation between local authorities in the use of freeing orders.[8] In three areas, Shire High, Shire Low and Metro Low, we were told that freeing orders were often sought in care proceedings (i.e. at the same time as seeking care orders). In other local authorities, notably the two London authorities, freeing for adoption was never mentioned in relation to childcare planning and appears not to be standard policy or practice.

2.3 Variation in social workers' awareness and understanding of policies

Despite the frequent absence of written policies, social workers in most areas had clear ideas about their local authority's standpoint as inferred from practice guidelines or from "office mythology" (i.e. passed on by word of mouth), especially in relation to the role of adoption in childcare

---

[7] See also the discussion at Chapter 3, para 3.3.

[8] This variation of agency use of the freeing for adoption provisions was noted in Lowe *et al* (1993) chapter 3, section 3.2.1 and predicted to continue (see para 5.1.1(a)). Under the Adoption and Children Bill, freeing for adoption will be replaced by placement orders and agreements.

planning. In London High, which is a local authority with no written policy, one social worker confidently stated:

Our policy is to find permanent placements for young people and when we think about permanency we always think about adoption.

Paradoxically, in Shire Low, where there were well-documented policies, we found that although the social workers knew the "policies", they were not necessarily aware that they had been documented. There was also evidence that, in certain specific areas of child care, social workers from all the sample areas were unclear as to whether or not a policy existed in their local authority, particularly in connection with concurrent planning, contingency planning and twin tracking. We found that in all six local authorities there was general confusion over these terms and what they were used for, especially in relation to twin tracking and concurrent planning. Very little was known about concurrent planning. This was often thought to be the same as twin tracking, except in Metro Low where they felt that children who had been placed under a pilot scheme had achieved permanency more quickly than they would have done in the "normal" way. However, with this planning it is difficult to recruit people who are prepared to take on "hard-to-place" children and so the children who have been placed using concurrent planning would probably have been successfully placed for adoption using the conventional route. As far as twin-track planning is concerned, some social workers felt that it was difficult to work with the birth parents without seeming to work behind their backs at the same time.

Most social workers thought that they used contingency planning in proceedings and care plans and termed it correctly. However, in Metro High the feeling was that contingency planning constituted having an emergency meeting after a plan has failed in order to conduct a postmortem to see if the plan could be salvaged or whether another long-term plan should be secured.

Social workers in London High said that they were unsure as to whether any written policy existed on foster carers adopting the child they were caring for. In Metro High some social workers were unaware of the local authority policy on adoption although in practice that authority had a high use of adoption. They were also unaware of any policy on rehabilitation, although it was always carried out in practice and there were written guidelines which had to be followed.

Contradictory or inconsistent policy

We have already noted that two areas (Shire Low and Metro Low), by monitoring work performance, discovered inconsistencies between their teams that were affecting policy. In Metro Low it was found that the team leaders' views were possibly influencing team decision-making more than the departmental view. This was leading to the fragmentation of policy. To address this issue the number of "patch teams" (so-called because they cover a patch or district) was being reduced from nine (seven patch teams plus two specialist teams) to three and a new Children's Services Division was created on 1 July 2000. There was a similar story in Shire Low. Originally, the teams in the five areas of that county were completely autonomous. This led to major variations of policy between them. Consequently, a Children's Panel, chaired by the same person (a Head of Service who liaises with district managers), was set up in all five areas to monitor all the long-term child cases. The establishment of this panel expedited progress and reduced drift. In the other local authorities there was little mention of individual team policies. Nevertheless, it is to be noted that in London Low a more hierarchical system with more central responsibility and less district autonomy had recently been introduced, while in Shire High there is a central post of Adoption Co-ordinator to whom all possible adoptions must be referred (though there is no equivalent for long-term fostering).

Social worker inexperience deters use of adoption

In several areas we were told that social workers who may not have had much or any experience of adoption were finding it difficult to get to grips with the procedure and hence avoided planning for its use.[9] In Shire High, with a full-time, knowledgeable Adoption Co-ordinator in post, the social workers' confidence in opting for adoption had increased. Now, whenever adoption becomes part of a permanency plan, the Co-ordinator

---

[9] For our findings about social workers' experience see Appendix, Tables A and B.

immediately becomes involved with the case. It was acknowledged in Shire Low that social workers who were unfamiliar with the adoption process needed support in order to negotiate what were considered to be "difficult" procedures. As mentioned above, Children's Panels in the five areas of the county have now been established. Part of the role of the Panels is to encourage social workers to grapple with these procedures. One senior manager told us that the number of adoptions coming before their supervisory panel was increasing because, she believed, social workers were feeling more confident about working their way through the process. This belief was confirmed by two of the social workers interviewed in this area. One said that the procedures for dealing with the family, the child and the court during the adoption process could be 'quite daunting' but it was now available on computer in a step-by-step format.

We were aware of two other authorities who kept a record of their adoption procedures in the form of a printed manual.

2.4 Case management governed by pragmatic considerations and "folklore" culture

Some local authorities (for example, Shire High) appeared not to be dogmatic in their approach to adoption and were aware of factors that may have to be taken into account when executing the long-term plan for the child. In contrast, other authorities (for example, London High) appeared to be more single minded so that all children, no matter what their age, needs or wishes, were always considered for adoption first. If no suitable adoptive family could be found after some time, the plan might be changed to long-term fostering as a "second-best" placement. In London Low the two team managers interviewed echoed these two contrasting approaches. One always favoured adoption for younger children whereas the other was more equivocal, her focus being on the importance of avoiding drift and delay and facing up to the reality of what was achievable.

3 Record-keeping

3.1 LAC Forms

In three of the six authorities the Looking After Children (LAC) forms were kept in the same file as other information on the case, for example, correspondence, financial documents and running records. But quite often we found that some, if not all, of these LAC forms were missing from the files, although this varied from office to office. We also discovered that in those areas where there were several children from one family who were being looked after, the LAC forms may not have been completed for each child and it would be necessary to "crib" information from the files for the other siblings.

In the other three authorities the LAC forms were kept in a separate ring-back folder and, in general, we found that most of the forms were present. In one of these authorities the introduction of the special LAC system was enforced and had to be in place following a recent SSI inspection that had put them on "special measures".

3.2 Criticisms of the LAC forms

The LAC forms themselves were thought by some social workers to be difficult to use, 'badly put together', and 'ill-conceived'. They thought that the Care Plan, although it should be written down, was too static and thus meaningless because such plans are very fluid. As far as the Review of Arrangements form was concerned it was useful as a means of promoting discussion but there was generally not enough space to record what needed to be said. For example, the reasons why a plan is not being achieved is seldom on record:

Maybe that should be built into the statutory review . . . to write down why the plan hasn't worked, or isn't working, or why the outcome hasn't been achieved yet.

In Shire Low a social worker thought the forms in use did not reflect the important reasons for the decision-making:

The forms reflect the here and now and they ensure that standards are kept, they ensure that the social workers are doing their job in terms of contact, support, in terms of the plan. They're just a checklist . . .

3.3 Findings

Case files in each of the six local authorities were checked to see if copies of the following documents could be located, namely, the Care Plan, the Review of Arrangements and Essential Information Record (EIR) Parts 1 and 2. Our overall findings are shown in **Table 32** below.

Table 32
Whether specific documents were found in the case file

	Care Plan		Review of Arrangements		EIR Part 1		EIR Part 2	
	No:	%	No:	%	No:	%	No:	%
Yes	171	(82%)	212	(96%)	153	(70%)	142	(65%)
No	39	(18%)	8	(4%)	67	(31%)	78	(36%)

Reviews of Arrangements and Care Plans were found in over 80 per cent of the case files examined. Thirty of the Care Plans found were the social services' own version, particularly in the Shire Authorities. Shire High had the highest percentage of missing Care Plans and Reviews of Arrangements, with 36 per cent (N = 16) and 11 per cent (N = 5) respectively.

Essential Information Records were much less in evidence however, with approximately one-third being absent. This was especially the case for the Shire Authorities, and Metro High. Indeed, nearly 80 per cent of the EIR Part 2s were missing in Shire Low, with 55 per cent missing in both Shire High and Metro High.

On closer analysis, it is apparent that the majority of the missing documentation related to children for whom the plan was neither long-term fostering nor adoption. Forty-one per cent of the missing Care Plans came from this group, as did all of the missing Reviews of Arrangements. A slightly greater proportion of the missing EIR Part 1s came from this group (33%), and 46 per cent of the missing EIR Part 2s (N = 31) were from this category. However, another important factor was the time the child had been looked after: the greater the length of time, the more often information was found to be missing, particularly in relation to the EIRs. Thus EIR Part 1s were missing for 36 per cent of the children who had been looked after for between two and five years, rising to 40 per cent of those looked after for five years and over. In each of these two age groups, 40 per cent of the EIR Part 2s were missing.

From our experience of looking at case files in the six local authorities we have to conclude that the record-keeping in some of these areas was poor. Our inspection revealed that the LAC forms were sometimes either incomplete or appeared to have been completed on a "post hoc" basis. In cases where the child had been in care for a long time we would be unlikely to find a Care Plan. Indeed, in one local authority we noted that there was a general paucity of Care Plans on file and, where we did find them, they were often not up-to-date and were confused and contradictory about such matters as the category of plan (for example, both "living with relatives/friends" and "long-term placement with foster carers" were used to describe a plan for the child who was being fostered by relatives) and the date of the plan. While in some authorities the reasons for the plan were fully explained, in others there was a minimum of information, so that it was well nigh impossible to deduce the reasoning behind the decision-making process. On the whole it is probably fair to say that, in cases where adoption was the plan, the files and documentation were in better shape than in cases where long-term fostering was the agreed option. This finding probably reflects the fact that adoption files and forms are scrutinised by the Adoption Panel and are needed in the court process.

Perhaps even more worrying was our finding that, in 26 cases where a comparison could be made between the reasons for the long-term plan recorded in the Care Plan in the case file and those given by social workers when interviewed about those cases, half did not match up. Indeed, while in eight cases there was some degree of association between the reasons cited in the Care Plan and those mentioned by the social worker, there was only a complete match in four cases. On the face of it this is a startling discrepancy. However, it might be explained by the generality of the reasons recorded in the case files as against the more detailed reasons offered by the social workers we interviewed.

3.4 General record-keeping

Team leaders and social workers seem to be aware that their recording of cases generally needs to be monitored more closely. One Director of Social Services admitted that in his authority record-keeping was not their strength. He suggested this may be due in part to the legacy of the social workers themselves who find it hard to keep records up to date and whose approach to this task is often 'muddly and woolly'. His view was that often social workers do not have the confidence to write down on forms the assessments that they make in their heads.

Occasionally, there were more serious omissions in records. We were particularly startled when, in one of the London Boroughs, a team leader confessed to finding that there was a file missing from one of the illustrative cases which we were discussing. This concerned a child who had been in care for some 10 years who had experienced a series of disrupted foster placements. When he was a baby, it was planned to place him for adoption. The authority's social services department then experienced a period of organisational turbulence and the child's file evidently went missing for the next two years. It is now not known what happened to him until the authority began actively to search for a new adoptive family when a new file was begun two years later. The social worker surmised, probably rightly, that these crucial missing years might contain the origins of the child's later serious attachment problems.

3.5 New record-keeping initiatives

Some authorities appear to be taking initiatives to improve their record-keeping. In London Low they were working towards having information relating to a child on their computer system which would make it useful for management planning purposes, not just for the collection of statutory information. One authority (Shire High) had tried to adapt the LAC forms to make them more user-friendly. They had attempted to reduce the burden for social workers having to complete all the paperwork required while at the same time setting minimum standards for information sharing. They believe that the Care Plan should be an assessment of need rather than one of resource and should be more like a working document that is shared with the families to improve communication. In another area, a social worker suggested that what was needed was a system of quarterly summaries to keep an accurate record of the reasons for decisions on brightly coloured paper that could be located easily within the file. This would help new social workers understand quickly what had happened in the case, what the authority's assessment was, and why particular decisions had been made at key stages in the child's care history.

3.6   The Directors' views on record-keeping

Since the core of our study was based on data extracted from local authority records, and since we had become concerned at the wide variations in recording practice that appeared to exist, we asked the Directors for their general views about recording. There were three aspects about which we were particularly concerned: first, the utility of the LAC record system; secondly, why it seems to be left to individual local authorities to work out their own particular recording system rather than complying with a uniform national system; and thirdly, why there is not a system of travelling records when children move from one authority to another.

The LAC recording system[10]
As one of the London Directors told us:
> It's certainly a much better system than existed before which was totally chaotic, non-standardised recording which nobody could follow. It's meant to help us refocus the objectives of the job so that people see that the paperwork isn't an end in itself, but a support for them to monitor how they are dealing with the case.

Nevertheless, the general view of the Directors echoed that of the social workers and seems to be that, while in concept the LAC system is excellent, in practice it is too complex and takes too long and many social workers find it off-putting. Here are two comments:
> It's superb in concept. It's very thorough and it gathers a wide range of information, but I think it's too laborious. It can take forever, and it

---

[10] We are aware that Professor Harriet Ward of Loughborough University is, in collaboration with the Dartington Social Research Unit, currently revising the LAC scheme.

does not allow enough exercise of professional judgement over which bits to focus on. It's a standardised, paper-based version while what we need is an IT Windows based system such as "Care First".

Another Director from a Shire authority considered the LAC system:
 . . . too cumbersome, repetitive and muscle-bound.

In one of the Metropolitan authorities the Director told us that the department was in the process of transferring the LAC system onto an IT system so that it can be 'on PC so that people won't have to do so much hand-written stuff'.

Directors seemed to disagree about whether the LAC system prompted social workers to record their professional thinking and analysis of children's needs sufficiently. One thought there should be a much simpler, more straightforward 'assessment framework as a review record which could be shared with the child's family'. And indeed, in his authority, efforts had been made to adapt the LAC system to do so.

Most agreed with our research observations that reasons for child placement decisions were often not recorded. One blamed the lack of attention given to this in training, commenting:
It's a very difficult thing to record well. It's very easy to record loads and loads and learn nothing. On the other hand, if you are really skilled, you can use a light touch and get all the really important things down. Good recording is the key to being able to assess risk, to see patterns of behaviour. It underpins and informs all good evidence-based social work practice.

Several of the Directors made the point that records could be very valuable to children and families themselves. As one said:
I occasionally get letters from people who want to see their earlier files. If our records don't say why certain decisions were made when they were in care it can be quite dreadful for them.

Another Director told us that she did not think the usual social work file was much use to children who might later in life want to see their records.

They aren't actually what young people who come back and talk to us want to see at all; definitely not a folder full of forms. What they want are letters and pictures. They're interested in videos and CDs. I think children of the future are not going to sit there and look at paper forms. When you go through a file with a child you realise what a very limited tool it is, given that it is their history.

Another told us that, as far as possible, he would like to see all records open to children and families so that, for example, when a social worker visited, the family would receive a record of what they and the social worker had discussed.

A national approach and travelling records
Most of the Directors appeared to agree with us that a uniform national system that was sufficiently user-friendly would be a good idea. As one said:

It's incredible that when recording is so important, there is not a national system of recording. Here we are talking about a very mobile population and it's a nightmare following them and finding out what has gone before from other authorities.

Another said:

In our area we have lots of borders with other counties and a lot of families move from one authority to another. Why shouldn't we have one record that transfers with them? In the health service we all have that. Why not for child care?

4 Shortcomings in training[11]

The qualification of social workers[12] varied. In one authority, Shire Low, there were some relatively inexperienced social workers although the ratio

---

[11] For the Government's proposals to improve training see the White Paper, op cit, paras 4.9–4.13.

[12] The White Paper, op cit, at para 2.14, noted that the basic social work course does not properly equip social workers to deal with issues concerning decisions for "permanence" for children.

of supervisors was quite high. However, here they have also recognised that different skills are required for long-term planning and for assessment. In London Low, basic grade social workers – Grades 2–4 – are employed in long-term care teams.[13] There is, however, a large turnover of staff with the result that many are newly qualified. There is also a heavy reliance on recruiting people from the Antipodes and South Africa, who not only have different training, cultural backgrounds and expectations of childcare practice, but who are also likely to be short-term "birds of passage". In Metro Low responsibility for cases is held by Grades 2 or 3 though there is much less turnover of staff.

The ongoing childcare training of social workers varied but seemed generally poor. One worker admitted that she did not know what the decision between long-term fostering and adoption could be based on – it was not something she had been taught or given much thought to. In another local authority training did not look at children's long-term needs.[14]

From our discussions with the social workers we found that more often than not they felt that their formal training had not equipped them adequately for the reality of childcare practice, in particular in the area of long-term planning for children. The following points stand out:

- Most have simply learned on the job from colleagues and, in the more well-resourced authorities, from ongoing in-service training. Some criticised their formal training for being too general and too theoretical, and others felt that it concentrated more on day-to-day planning arrangements and how to process paper work according to guidelines than on increasing their understanding of long-term childcare issues.
- One team manager thought that social workers were no longer trained in record-keeping skills and lacked the academic and intellectual ability to understand what they were doing. We were told that new

---

[13] For further information about the experience of social workers, see Appendix, Tables A and B.

[14] This issue is also discussed in the White Paper, ibid at para 5.23, where it is proposed to improve post-qualification training for social workers by establishing a new Post-Qualifying Award in Child Care.

social workers had often not experienced statutory placements on their training courses and therefore had little idea what statutory child care meant.

- A team leader from London High felt that in his authority there was a noticeable divide between the childcare teams and the family-finding unit which led to gaps in overall knowledge of how their long-term childcare planning operated.

- In some areas we were told that it had only recently been recognised that particular skills and knowledge were required for long-term planning and the assessment of children, for example, in subjects such as mental health. In at least two authorities (Shire Low and Shire High) key workers with this kind of experience and knowledge were being recruited in order to broaden the overall perspectives of those involved in child placement planning.

5 The Directors' views of staff recruitment and development

Directors were asked for their views of the training required for effective child placement decision-making and whether their authorities had a continuing professional development strategy for this kind of work.

In one of the better resourced authorities, we were told that:

All the fieldwork staff are qualified in either Diploma in Social Work or Certificate in Qualification of Social Work depending on how old they are. There are a number of staff going through post-qualifying training at the moment. Our first 10 will be completing their first level of post-qualifying at the end of the month.

This particular authority also had an in-house childcare training programme for staff as well as a relatively small budget to allow staff to go on external courses at various times designed to fit in with a system of individualised professional development which is completed on every member of staff annually.

One of the London authorities had a long tradition of close involvement with various university social work courses. In the past this seems to have facilitated the recruitment and retention of well-trained childcare staff.

The Director saw the encouragement of continuing professional education as an important part of a staff retention "package", as were their general working relationships with specialist childcare treatment organisations like the Great Ormond Street Hospital and the Tavistock Institute. Even so, the high cost of living in London and what she reported as the relatively low pay which newly-qualified social workers receive was now creating something of a recruitment and staff retention problem. She reported that 'For the first time we have more leavers than starters'.

The newly appointed Director of the other London authority, now emerging from its adverse SSI inspection, was less fortunate with respect to staff recruitment. While the department was in crisis there were severe staff shortages and considerable use of short-term agency staff. As the new Director told us:

If you talked to the children they would tell you the familiar story that their social worker changed every three months. Up until recently there was an average stay of 22 weeks for 50 per cent of the staff. It is not an exaggeration to say that you would meet children who had been allocated a social worker who had left before they had met them.

This authority had attempted to improve staff stability. As the Director said:

That's good news, but it's not altogether what it may seem because you can put people on short-term contracts instead of being agency staff. This is not untypical. We will have taken on three South African social workers through an agency and put them on short-term contracts guaranteeing them six to nine months work. In the sense of temporary agency staff they are off the books but turnover is only marginally lower than it would have been if they had been straight agency staff. The situation has stabilised a lot but if you were looking at staff and thinking of a reasonable span – say five years – working with the same cases, you would find that a rarity.

This Director, having previously worked in a different part of the country, told us she had been quite shocked by the staffing problems she had found in London. Recently they had 13 Diploma in Social Work students on a three-month placement at the end of which she had asked them whether they would like to work in the department. She told us:

Every one of them said they would go and work in an agency. I asked them why when we could offer them a permanent job. Do you know what they replied? 'We are not sure we want to work in this particular field of social work. Working for an agency we can dip in and out.' You see they didn't want to accept responsibility if anything went wrong. What they meant was that if you get into a very deep situation in a case, you didn't have to come in next Monday and deal with it. You could say to the agency: 'I'll go somewhere else now.'

This disturbing verbatim observation from a highly experienced Director of Social Services really does take us to the heart of the matter. How can we expect careful, well-considered childcare decisions based on sound research-based evidence and a proper understanding of individual children's needs to be taken in authorities which experience such serious childcare staffing problems? And what is it that lies at the root of these staffing problems? Not just, we would suggest, the problems of social work pay and the high cost of housing in London, important though these are. If the reality is as this Director told us, there is a very serious and perhaps more fundamental problem of acute anxiety on the part of front-line fieldworkers dealing with childcare decisions, which may well reflect a serious lack of professional confidence. Evidence for this view came from another Director in one of the shire authorities with over 20 years childcare experience who suggested that this malaise could be traced to two major causes: first, to the cumulative effect of the publicity given to child abuse scandals over the last decade or so. As he said:

Social workers have had a bad press for a long time so it is difficult to feel confident and assertive as a professional.

Secondly, he pointed to what he regarded as a deterioration in the quality of childcare social work training:

I would say that there has been a dumbing-down of social work training and social work skills. We take on newly trained social workers who do not have a working knowledge of child development. Now social work practice is all "process" – it's all too clockwork – doing

things by the management manual. I think there has been a disinvestment by Government over a long time in social work training.
It's not for nothing that training courses are not full. It's part of the erosion of the profession.

Good childcare training based on sound knowledge and carefully supervised staff, he considered:
. . . is all about equipping our staff – it motivates staff, it attracts staff, it keeps staff here, it keeps the profession alive. It keeps the respect of other professions and the confidence of the elected members. It is a vital part of workforce planning.

The point which he made about social work having become fixated with process was echoed by one of the London Directors who told us:
Social workers have become obsessed with process rather than outcome. The reviews are about ensuring that you have ticked the box saying you have visited the child beforehand and that they have got their medical. Then you go to the review and the review takes place and then you start ticking the boxes again. Social workers seem to have forgotten what their role in childcare is. It's about having that very special relationship with the child and the family.

She went on to tell us that before she took up the Director's role in this particular authority, she had spent four weeks observing what went on in the Looked After Children Team of another authority with a sufficiently good professional reputation. She was shocked by what she saw:
I was stunned by seeing people sat at their desks making phone calls, filling in forms and hardly ever seeing a child. I thought I couldn't tolerate this if I was them. I'd see the child first and then fill in the forms. It is almost entirely the other way around. If you talk to people about how much contact they'd had literally in the six months between reviews, if it was four occasions they were thought to be really good social workers. That's the reality of what social work childcare practice is about just now, I'm afraid. If I wanted social workers to be entirely process focused and bureaucratic, I'd employ different people because other people are much more efficient at it than social workers who

*don't come into the job to process paper and are therefore often
reluctant to do it.*

6 Management structure and organisation

Local authorities have a discretion to organise their social service
departments how they wish, provided that their statutory responsibilities
can be discharged. Many considerations determine how this is done. Each
of our six authorities had designed their own particular arrangements. As
discussed earlier,[15] we were told by three authorities that their management
structures had recently been reorganised with a view to providing a more
consistent approach to childcare planning. We have written extensively
elsewhere (see Lowe and Murch *et al*, 1999, pp. 401–26) about such
questions as: how adoption services are organised by local authorities,
referring, for example, to the pros and cons of centralised or de-centralised
teams; the relationship between district social workers and managers; and
the problems posed by hierarchical and attenuated chains of command.
Here it is only necessary to mention that this more recent study confirms
many of the earlier findings. The picture gained is that all authorities
have extensive hierarchical management structures with various tiers of
appointment (some specialist) above the fieldwork social workers who
invariably work in teams of various kinds (i.e. some in general placement
teams, some within specialist adoption teams, others in general child care
or across-the-board social work patch teams). In some, the basic grade
social workers reported to senior social workers. Team leaders or managers
generally occupy a tier above, with some carrying out supervision and
others not. One team manager in London Low questioned her role. She
thought it was now seen as a business and financial post and less of a
senior practitioner post. A person with little experience of social work
practice could now be appointed as team manager. In Shire High there
was a further tier of service manager who supervises the team leaders
within one area office.

We found that there were mixed views about the change to independent
chairs for reviews. One social worker in London Low thought that an

---

[15] See Chapter 3, para 4.2.

independent chair made the whole process of review rather 'formulaic' because the decision-maker was now not present. On the other hand, the change was favoured in Shire High because there was now pressure from the independent chair to get the report written and sent to the parents before the review.

7 Directors' personal involvement in childcare policy-making

It was noticeable that the Directors varied a good deal in how far they appeared to involve themselves directly in the authority's childcare work.

In one authority a Director, recently appointed as something of a "hands-on trouble shooter" following a critical SSI report of the authority's childcare work, told us that she regarded it as an important part of her job to have direct involvement with accommodated children and to regularly listen to their views. With the support of the authority's Chief Executive and the Chair of Social Services, she had instituted a number of measures which directly involved children, such as the appointment of children's representatives to the authority's Corporate Parent Panel which, following the Quality Protects initiative, takes serious policy decisions. We were told how the children's representatives on the panel had influenced the members in decisions to provide grants to support and encourage accommodated children through higher education and to pay for a proportion of the costs of driving lessons. As she said:

From our point of view it's a very vital way of ensuring members know what is going on in the childcare system.

In contrast, in some of the other authorities the Directors seemed to have delegated much of the authority's childcare policy to their deputies and other middle managers at various levels. Our impression was, however, that authorities generally were becoming more aware of the need for management at all levels to put in place more effective mechanisms to monitor the progress and development of looked after children.

8 Summary

The following points emerged from our interviews with the 26 social workers and the Directors in the six sample authorities.

8.1 Response to the Quality Protects Programme

- All the Directors valued the Government's Quality Protects initiative – it had been a valuable spur to action in a number of respects and stimulated a number of new local childcare initiatives.
- But it had resulted inadvertently in the following problems:
  - It had "siphoned off" some good experienced fieldwork staff into new specific posts thereby weakening the front line.
  - The unresolved question of whether the new Quality Protects money was a one-off exercise or was to be permanent made long-term planning difficult.[16]

8.2 Policy problems

The study revealed a number of issues relating to placement policies.
- Few authorities had written policy statements which explained the reasons for policy.
- Some had no written policy about permanence at all.
- There was considerable variation and confusion between and within local authorities concerning the factors to be taken into account when planning the long-term future of looked after children, particularly concerning the following key issues:
  - when to abandon attempts at rehabilitation;
  - how to avoid drift and the possible use of timescales;
  - whether to place children with extended family;
  - whether to permit adoption by foster carers;
  - whether to use the freeing procedure in adoption.

---

[16] It was announced on 20 March 2002 that the Quality Protects Programme has been extended from three years to five years with funding increased from £375m to £885m: Press Release: reference 2002/0145.

8.3 Social workers' awareness, understanding and application of placement policies

- Although most social workers had a clear idea what the authority's permanent placement policy was, there were certain areas of confusion concerning concurrent planning, contingency planning and twin tracking.
- In some places social workers' inexperience of procedure deterred the use of adoption.

8.4 Record-keeping

- In the Stage 2 sample of 220 children a number of essential documents could not be located in the case files, thus,
  - 18% had no Care Plan;
  - 31% had no Essential Information Record Part 1;
  - 36% had no Essential Information Record Part 2;
  - 4% contained no evidence of a statutory review.
- But it was apparent that the majority of the missing documentation related to children for whom the plan was neither adoption nor long-term fostering.
- The greater the length of time that the child had been looked after, the more often information was found to be missing, particularly in relation to the Essential Information Records.

8.5 Use of Looking After Children (LAC) forms

- In some places these were kept in the child's file, in other areas separately.
- There was wide variation in how well these forms had been filled in between and within local authorities.
- Some were incomplete. Others had been filled in on a "post hoc" basis.
- In a number of instances it was not possible to deduce from the information in the file and/or the LAC forms what the reasons for the permanency placement decisions were.
- Some social workers and Directors criticised the LAC forms as being too cumbersome and not user-friendly.

- The study revealed a need for:
    i) A new modern, uniform, national system of recording.
    ii) A record that travelled with children if they moved to the care of other authorities.

8.6 Shortcomings in training

Social workers and Directors felt that formal social work training had many deficiencies when it came to preparing staff for childcare practice. In particular:
- inadequate skill and knowledge required for long-term planning and assessment of children;
- how to keep good records.

8.7 Staff recruitment and retention

A number of Directors, particularly in the London and the Metropolitan authorities, expressed grave concern about the ability to recruit and retain qualified staff, drawing attention to the deterrent factors of:
- low morale;
- the risks and dangers of missing serious child abuse;
- low pay and the high cost of housing, particularly in London;
- a lack of professional stimulation due to an excessive preoccupation with bureaucratic processes.

References

Lowe N with Borkowski M, Copner R, Griew K and Murch M (1993), *Report of the Research into the Use and Practice of the Freeing for Adoption Provisions*, London: HMSO

Lowe N and Murch M, Borkowski M, Weaver A, Beckford V with Thomas C (1999), *Supporting Adoption – Reframing the approach*, London: BAAF

Part III

Issues for concern

6 Conclusions and recommendations

It is not our intention in this final chapter to summarise all our findings. Instead we propose to concentrate first on a few key findings and then on what we see as wider matters of concern raised by this research.

1 Defining high and low use of adoption

As we said at the beginning of this report, the aims of the study were two-fold:

1. to examine the process which determined whether a looked after child is fostered or adopted and to investigate possible reasons for a wide variation in local authorities' use of adoption; and
2. to examine the issue of "delay" in the adoption and long-term fostering process, investigating what measures local authorities have introduced to identify and combat causes of delay.

The former aim was based on the premise that because, according to national statistics,[1] there were some authorities who seemed to be "high users" of adoption but others who were "low users", investigation was required to explain this apparent discrepancy. With this in mind we selected for our investigation three appropriately matched pairs of authorities based upon their high and low use of adoption. For these purposes "high use" was defined as being more than 5.6 per cent of the looked after population who were adopted and "low use" as being below 2.7 per cent of the looked after population in the authority. What our detailed investigation revealed, however, was that, by selecting a cohort of children for whom a choice between long-term fostering or adoption was a serious possibility (namely, those aged between one and 12 years

---

[1] Viz the Department of Health PAF Indicator C23 percentage of children looked after who were adopted from local authority care, 1998. But note this Indicator has since been amended – see below.

who had already been looked after for a continuous period of 12 months or who had experienced three or more distinct episodes of being or ceasing to be looked after during that time), the proportions of those for whom adoption was the long-term plan was quite different. On this analysis the proportion for whom adoption was the plan ranged from 45 per cent in London High to 17 per cent in Shire Low.[2] More importantly, we found that at 42 per cent, London Low was not only substantially higher than Metro High at 30 per cent but twice as high as Shire High at 21 per cent. Even when analysing those children actually placed for adoption at 31 March 2000,[3] London Low was still found to place proportionally more children than Shire High.

This analysis clearly brought into question the value and correctness of the PAF Indicator as it was originally conceived (though ironically, this Indicator correctly identified high and low use as between *types* of authority at any rate within the six investigated in this project). It was accordingly our view that, insofar as an Indicator is thought necessary to assess the scale of adoptions (but we should make it clear that we do not share the view that it is appropriate to regard adoption figures as necessarily indicating good, bad or indifferent practice – that seems to us to be too crude a measure upon which to evaluate local authorities' child placement performance)[4] then bearing in mind that nearly half of looked after children are returned home within eight weeks, some attention needs to be paid to the length of time the child has been looked after. We therefore suggested in our report to the Department of Health that only those who have been "continuously" looked after for six months or more should be included and, ideally, even then there should be a filter mechanism to screen out those for whom rehabilitation is a key part of the plan. In other words, it was, in our view, both simpler and fairer only to include in the base-line measure all children who have been looked after continuously for six months and for whom the plan is not to return to their birth family (the main options being: continuing to live with

---

[2] See Table 11 in Chapter 2 at para 2.1.

[3] See Table 13 in Chapter 2 at para 3.4.

[4] Cf Barth (1999) 'Setting performance goals for adoption services: estimating the need for adoption of children in foster care' *Adoption Quarterly* Vol 2 (3), cited in the Prime Minister's *Review of Adoption*, op cit, Annex 7 at 87.

extended birth family/relatives; long-term fostering; adoption; residential care; and residential education). We were also critical of the Indicator for its failure to take into account such factors as variations in the size of the local authority and related measures of social deprivation, its child population and varying use of options *other* than adoption including respite care. Finally, we pointed out that as cases vary from year to year, reliance on a one-year snapshot was potentially misleading[5] and that at the very least, regard should be given to statistics over a three-year period.

Since submitting our Report to the Department of Health, the PAF Indicator has been changed in that the denominator now (that is, for 2001 – 2002) only includes children looked after for six months or more rather than all looked after children. As the Local Authority Circular states:[6]

This will increase the usefulness of the indicator as it will no longer include those children looked after for a short time before returning home for whom adoption would not be appropriate.

This change clearly goes some way to addressing our concerns. Moreover, it must be added that the Indicator is currently under review. The Department of Health has also pointed out that in any event the Indicator does not provide the sole criterion by which local authority performance is judged, rather it acts as a trigger for possible further investigation.

2 Key factors in determining the long-term plans

Notwithstanding our criticisms of the PAF Indicator, it remains the case that we found wide variations in the local authorities' use of adoption. However, it is not easy to explain why there were such variations since there seemed to be general agreement, at any rate, on the key determinants of what the long-term plan should be for a looked after child who is not returning home. Furthermore, we found little evidence of written policy advocating adoption over long-term fostering or vice versa in any of the authorities we visited. However, from anecdotal evidence in interviews we were able to deduce that some local authorities, for example, London High, have clear policies prescribing adoption.

---

[5] See further, the discussion in Chapter 2 at para 3.2.

[6] See LAC (2001) 33.

Of course, in determining the long-term plan for any child there will in practice be a whole range of factors to be taken into account but, when considered in isolation, the two (not unrelated) most important factors were the child's age and the level of contact with the birth family. With regard to the former we found that the overall age profile of the child at the time when he or she last started to be looked after and for whom adoption was the plan, was significantly lower than for those children for whom long-term fostering was the plan. The younger the child when he or she last started to be looked after, the more likely there would be a plan for adoption made for that child.

However, if the age of the child was the only determining factor when planning for long-term care, one would expect the "high use" authorities to have a higher proportion of younger children (under five years old) than "low use" authorities. This was not the case in our study where analysis of the data revealed that, in general, in "high use" authorities children were older at the start of their last episode of being looked after than children in "low use" authorities with the exception of one authority, Metro High. London Low had a greater proportion of younger children (1–4 years old) being looked after than the national average. We have to conclude that there must be other factors that are part of the equation. In this regard, an interesting finding[7] was that girls were more likely than boys to have a plan for adoption, especially if they were in the younger age group. However, the local authorities in our sample all had a greater proportion of boys to girls than the national average of looked after children, with the exception of Metro Low. "Low use" authorities would be expected to have a greater percentage of looked after boys to girls than "high use" authorities if gender was a significant factor in long-term planning; this is not so in our study.

The second major factor, as we have said, is the level of contact between the child and his or her birth family. In this regard we found[8] that the older child who had more contact with his or her birth family was more likely to have a long-term fostering plan. This plan would allow that contact to be maintained. However, we also found[9] that the age of the

---

[7] See Chapter 3, para 2.2.
[8] See Chapter 3, para 2.1.
[9] See Chapter 3, para 3.4.

child was probably more of a primary consideration than contact with the birth family, especially when decisions on long-term care have to be made for younger children. Social workers thought that the relationship between the child and the birth parents was significant and if there was a chance of rehabilitation, albeit not in the immediate future, then long-term fostering would be the most likely option in the Care Plan.

We found that two other factors tended to militate against planning for adoption. First, it appears from our study[10] that looked after children from minority ethnic backgrounds and for whom returning home was no longer an option, were more likely to end up in a long-term fostering placement than to be adopted, either by design or default. This is clearly an important finding which deserves further investigation.

Secondly, looked after children with emotional and/or behavioural problems or who had been severely abused, were more likely to be subject to plans for long-term fostering.[11] The reasons for choosing this option are primarily related to the child's perceived inability to form attachments and the consequent level of therapeutic and possibly financial support that would be required by the child's potential carer.

The issues surrounding these children who are "hard to place" are inextricably linked with the availability of resources and the degree of support, financial and otherwise, that can be offered. Social workers in some authorities thought that the scarcity of suitable adopters and long-term foster carers sometimes caused changes to be made to the child's original Care Plan. The ideal plan, in terms of the best interests of the child, may have been tempered with what is available in terms of resources. The extent of support that is on offer to the potential carer may also affect the planned outcome.

It might also be added that the quite understandable reluctance to plan adoption for "hard-to-place" children pays no heed to whether the alternative of long-term fostering offers a better or at least no worse an option for the child.

---

[10] See Chapter 3, para 2.3.
[11] See Chapter 3, para.2.9.

3 Duration of the process

The second aim of the project was to examine the issue of delay in the adoption and long-term fostering process. In this respect we point out that a key element in the duration of the process is the time spent on rehabilitation. Yet there appears to be no national policy on the issues surrounding rehabilitation, for example, how long rehabilitation should be attempted before a decision is made that the child will no longer be able to return home. Indeed, only Shire Low out of the six authorities we investigated appeared to have a clear policy about monitoring attempts at rehabilitation to avoid drift. It appears that in most instances each case is judged individually according to the circumstances, although at least one local authority is taking steps to introduce set timescales. Generally, we found[12] that attempts at rehabilitation lasted well over one year for children for whom adoption became the plan and a period of two years for children where long-term fostering became the plan. We recommend that urgent consideration be given to issuing national guidance on rehabilitation issues.

Once the plan for adoption had been made, we found[13] that matching the child to suitable adopters took around nine months. In cases where long-term fostering was planned, the matching process was slightly quicker, around four months on average. Overall, we found[14] that, on average, nearly two years had elapsed between deciding on a plan for adoption and the granting of an adoption order. Furthermore, children for whom adoption was the plan waited just over three years altogether from the time they last started to be looked after until they were adopted. We have suggested that three years in a young child's life is too long a time to wait for stability. The LAC (98) 20 targets have proposed that a child for whom adoption is the plan should wait no longer than 19 months from the start of being looked after until being adopted,[15] but it is clear, judging on our findings, that this is likely to prove a tough aspiration. In our view

---

[12] See Chapter 4, para 3.3.
[13] See Chapter 4, para 5.
[14] See Chapter 4, para 5.
[15] See also the timescales to be introduced by *National Standards for Adoption in England*, discussed at Chapter 5, para 2.2.

there is an evident need to improve the monitoring and periodic review of each child's placement. This is necessary in order to "inoculate" accommodated children against the lurking and enduring problem of drift. We have seen how various authorities are taking initiatives in this matter – the appointment of children's review panels, special officers to monitor case progress regularly, "trigger" mechanisms and the like. These new anti-drift procedures need to be evaluated around the country in order to see what works best.

4 The issue of multiple placements

One of the more disturbing findings[16] was that around one-third of children for whom adoption or long-term fostering was the plan, had experienced four or more placement moves. We also noted variations between local authorities in this respect and found that children for whom adoption was the plan, even though younger on average, had experienced more placement moves since being looked after than children for whom long-term fostering was the plan.

As a research team we remain deeply concerned about the problem of multiple short-term placements particularly for very young children.[17] There are major mental health implications here for their capacity to form secure trusting attachments. In addition, multiple placements seriously risk disrupting children's schooling with consequent knock-on effects on their educational attainment. In the past we have called – without effect – for research to quantify the scale of this problem and to identify those areas where it is most serious. For example, how many moves do children experience when on a series of interim care orders? What is the correlation between the length of the planning process and the number of moves? How do local authorities and court areas vary in this regard? Is the problem getting better or worse? What are the consequences for the child

---

[16] See Chapter 4, para 6.

[17] Concern evidently shared by the Government. See the White Paper, ibid, at para 2.3. We note also with concern that the recent Department of Health Report (2000) *Tracking Progress in Children's Services: An evaluation of local responses to the Quality Protects Programme – year 2* (at p. 31) reports that, with regard to placement stability, returns from councils indicated 'no significant change in the average position over the previous year'.

and for the stability of later long-term options, whether foster care or adoption? We recommend that these issues be added to the list of researchable topics highlighted by the Adoption White Paper[18] and which the Government intends to fund.

5 Wider considerations and recommendations

Having summarised our main findings we conclude this report with what seem to us to be the main implications for future policy and practice.

Although we had two specific objectives, first, to explore the factors associated with placement choice and second, to study the duration of the process and the issue of "delay", we quickly came to realise that it was not possible to understand these matters without considering their wider context. This inevitably has included such questions as: the way local authority child placement services are organised; the nature of their policies and how these are communicated to their staff; the social workers' knowledge, understanding and experience of childcare work and whether or not the system facilitates or hinders the application of this vital staff resource in the service of children in need. But first, we should preface our conclusions by summarising what we see as the overall objective of the child placement task since this is the basic yardstick by which we have come to evaluate the services that we have been studying.

5.1 The goal of child placement

When considering placement choice for children in need of long-term care, whether it be via fostering or adoption, the goal of local authorities must surely be to provide the child with a supportive, stable family environment as soon as possible. Indeed the first objective of the Government's plans for children's social services[19] is 'to ensure that children are securely attached to carers capable of providing safe and effective care for the duration of childhood'. The return of stability to their lives should

---

[18] Ibid, at para 7.10.

[19] See Department of Health (2000) *Tracking Progress in Children's Services – an Evaluation of local responses to the Quality Protects Programme – Year 2*, Appendix 1 at p. 105.

be the top priority for children who, in the context of deteriorating home circumstances often associated with abuse, neglect and violence, have experienced much uncertainty and flux and who, in the initial stages of being cared for by local authorities, might have had to move several times from one foster home to another. It seems to us that it is often forgotten that the use of the rhetoric of permanence can be easily interpreted by the children and their birth family as a threat to sever kinship ties which are important for the child's identity. Practitioners need, particularly with respect to the adoption of older children out of care, to stress the importance of the desired stability of future arrangements rather than the severance connotations associated with adoption.

6 The need to consider the full spectrum of options

Taking the choice of the child issue first, it is clear that the study has highlighted the crucial importance of considering the full spectrum of options when planning for children. Many factors determine whether or not adoption should be preferred to long-term fostering or vice versa. The current media and political interest in adoption risks diverting attention from the important fostering option where, as we have seen, there are many worrying aspects (such as inconsistent allowances, recruitment difficulties, lack of professional support, etc). It may also fail to encourage social workers to consider the option of placement with other relatives which other studies (see Harwin and Owen, 2002; Rowe *et al*, 1984) have shown to have relatively good outcomes.[20]

7 The need to eliminate current disincentives to long-term fostering

One clear conclusion we have reached is that, in terms of planning for children, long-term fostering has become something of a Cinderella option – certainly in comparison with adoption. A number of informants told us of the difficulties they had in recruiting and retaining long-term foster carers. Finding adoptive homes was difficult enough but discovering good foster

---

[20] This range of options will be further extended when the provisions under the Adoption and Children Bill for special guardianship are introduced.

homes was even harder. The reasons suggested included the stigma associated with local authority "welfarism"; lower allowances for long-term carers in some authorities in comparison with short-term rates; the problems of coping with contact with disturbed and sometimes aggressive birth families; the lack of stability in the foster care structure where children may be short-stay birds of passage; and the general problems of coping with older children who might exhibit distressed, disturbed and challenging behaviour (including unfounded allegations of abuse). There was also sometimes an implication in what the social workers told us that they and their colleagues could not guarantee the degree of support and encouragement that foster carers needed, particularly at times of crisis. Ironically, most if not all of these problems are also associated with adoption and indeed the lack of a post-adoption service has dissuaded some authorities from considering adoption as an option for some children.[21]

It seems from this research that while short-term fostering with a view to rehabilitation, on the one hand, and adoption on the other, are reasonably well understood, the term "long-term fostering" is imprecise. For example, at what point does a placement become "long-term"? How definite must it be that the child will not be returning home? Such imprecision reflects the indeterminate nature of the law concerning fostering.[22] Furthermore, it is hard to find *positive* policies concerning its use. Moreover, these problems seem likely to us to be further exacerbated by the proposed introduction of the special guardianship provisions under the Adoption and Children Bill.

7.1 Prioritising adoption – to the detriment of long-term fostering?

One of the obvious dangers of prioritising adoption is that it concentrates too much energy and resources (for example, in recruiting potential adopters and supporting adoptive placements) into what, after all, is a small percentage of the looked after children to the detriment of other children – especially older children for whom adoption is much less likely

---

[21] See the findings of Lowe and Murch *et al*, 1999.

[22] See the discussion in Chapter 2, para 2.

to be thought of as an option.[23] Although we must emphasise that we have no evidence of misuse of adoption, there is a danger that authorities, keen to meet their percentage target for adoption, may too hastily rule out rehabilitation with the birth parents or wider family, particularly for young children who are likely to be thought more adoptable. It could also introduce complacency among those authorities who either meet their targets or who have reached their target in a particular year.

As we have previously intimated, there seems widespread confusion as to exactly what is meant by long-term fostering. It tends to be spoken of rather negatively in the sense that it is referred to when adoption is ruled out and when no obvious return to the family is foreseen. In these types of cases it seems to be regarded as the residual option where none other is suitable. Alternatively, it comes about reactively to earlier placements; perhaps the child and foster carers have clearly bonded but the foster carers do not want to adopt. The impression we gained from some authorities was that long-term foster care was seen as a lower status of caring than adoption.

What we would like to see is a future initiative on long-term fostering to complement what has been done for adoption. In our view, there needs to be an overall nationally co-ordinated coherent policy for *all* children who are not going home – both for adoption and long-term fostering. There is a need for policy and planning for long-term fostering to be sharpened up – with clear answers as to what it is and *positive* reasons for its use.

7.2 The need for a stronger national co-ordination of child placement policy

Moving onto the broader contextual issues highlighted by this study, we have been struck by the extraordinary degree of policy and practice variation that exists between local authorities. In this field, each authority

---

[23] An attempt to tackle this is made by the provisions in the Adoption and Children Bill to create a "special guardianship" status which is intended to provide for "permanence" but which would not involve the *legal* separation involved in adoption. It remains to be seen whether these provisions will simply add further complications or whether they will make a positive difference.

invents its own childcare management system, designs its own practice guidelines and sets out its policies (whether written or not) in its own idiosyncratic way (providing endless scope for research!). All this must involve a considerable degree of costly managerial duplication around the country and lead to much confusion for practitioners and public alike. This prompts us to question:

- why there should be this variation; and
- whose responsibility is it?

Is it sensible to leave local authorities to their own devices? Is it not a waste of resources in any event to have each authority drawing up its own policy? What needs to be sorted out is what is of national concern and what is of local concern. There are many areas – record-keeping is perhaps the most obvious, the collation of statistics another and also variations in allowances – where a more uniform national system is required. We think the time is long overdue when Government needs to consider what should be done at the central level and what should be delegated more appropriately to local government, assuming for the time being that childcare services continue in local authority hands.[24]

8 Problems of record-keeping

We have already discussed[25] the varying quality of record-keeping – not all authorities used the LAC forms and even in those that did, not all were complete. Often the reasons for decisions were brief or even formulaic.[26] Indeed, we gained the strong impression that recording often occurred long after the event instead of being reasonably con-temporaneous. We learned of some examples of "doctoring" or, at any rate, "tidying up" of the files ahead of social service inspections and even of our research! On occasion the information was contradictory. This varying quality and reliability not only had knock-on consequences for our research (inasmuch as the qualitative data collected from the case

---

[24] We acknowledge that some of these problems are addressed by the introduction of National Standards for Adoption.

[25] See above Chapter 2, para 5.3.

[26] For example, that adoption was in the child's best interests.

files did not include the decision-making process in as much detail as had been hoped, though, as we have seen,[27] that process was illuminated further by our practitioner interviews), but has much wider implications.

- First, if the knowledge of how these decisions on long-term fostering or adoption are reached is known to the social worker but not fully recorded on the files, there is the obvious danger that if social workers leave the authority, then a lot of this knowledge will leave with them. A new social worker, faced with incomplete or even inaccurate or contradictory information could well jump to the wrong conclusion about what is supposed to be happening in the case. In any event, the absence of reliable information on the files must, on occasion, jeopardise an authority's ability to monitor the child's progress and so contribute to his or her "drift" in care.

- Secondly, inadequate record-keeping may prevent other workers from seeing an overall pattern which may be vital to the child's or other children's (e.g. siblings) protection. A reported case in point is *Re E* (*Care Proceedings: Social Work Practice,*)[28] in which five children of a family had been subjected to constant emotional, physical and sexual abuse over a 20-year period and in which there had been a history of ineffectual social work intervention accompanied by the family's failure to co-operate with the professionals. The files were over four-feet high. The importance of this case lies in Bracewell J's closing remarks in which she set out a number of principles including:

  - Every social work file should have as its top document a running chronology of significant events which is kept up to date. (In this case it was only when the newly assigned social worker went through the 'jumbled mass' of documents, that the cyclical pattern of abuse became so apparent as to justify immediate action.)

  - Line managers and those with the power to make decisions, should never make a judgment to take no action without having full knowledge of the file and consulting with those professionals who know the family.

---

[27] See above, Chapter 2, para 3.1.

[28] [2000] 2 FLR 254. We came across two comparable cases in our own research sample.

- Children who are part of a sibling group should not be considered in isolation but should be considered in the context of family history. Where previous children have been brought to the attention of social services, details of their cases should be considered in assessing what went wrong historically and whether appropriate change had been effected. As Bracewell J put it, 'History has a habit of repeating itself in a recognisable pattern, as in this case'.
- Working or attempting to work with the family must be time limited.

These eminently sensible guidelines are clearly dependent on accurate, contemporaneous and full records.

- Thirdly, the absence of detailed records of decision-making will certainly make it difficult for children themselves to understand them if, in later life, they choose to look at the files. This must surely have human rights implications[29] which, of course, is now of particular importance since the implementation of the Human Rights Act 1998.
- Fourthly, the danger of ex post facto reasoning is that they might well amount to defensive or even aspirational accounts by the social workers.
- Fifthly, in the absence of reliable records, how can local authorities produce accurate statistics upon which national policy is so dependent?

What, if anything, can be done about this problem?[30] First, the realities of the work place have to be acknowledged. Social workers are commonly overworked and having to deal with crises. For them record-keeping is a chore and will commonly be accorded a low priority. It is vital to instil a new culture in which record-keeping is regarded as a key tool. It should accordingly be part of basic training. Management should insist on contemporaneous record-keeping and allow time for it to be done. At the same time forms should be made simple. We have plenty of evidence that

---

[29] For example, in connection with a claim by a parent or a child that local authority action amounted to an unjustified interference with the right to respect for private and family life contrary to Article 8.

[30] See also the Government's proposals in the White Paper, ibid, at paras 7.8 et seq.

the LAC forms (which we understand are under review) are not user-friendly: much of the information required is repetitive which not only adds to the drudgery of their completion but is wasteful of valuable social worker time. They should be simplified, but in a uniform way. One authority, Shire High, has significantly adapted the forms to make them more user-friendly. Other authorities, for example, Metro High and Metro Low in our sample, supplemented the forms by having their own more detailed individual records of review. While this shows commendable (though time-consuming) initiative, such local individualism makes for overall complexity.

Another complication is both the varied extent to which local authorities are computerised and the fact that they use different systems and suppliers. It would clearly be helpful if all authorities were computerised and used compatible systems. Indeed, it is vital, if they are to be more readily able to transfer information about children who move from one area to another.

The overall objective should be to create a National Standard System of childcare recording, ideally computer-based, so that as well as being an essential practice tool for social workers, management information can also be obtained.[31] This should always include the Care Plans and Essential Information Records; a concise day-to-day chronology charting key developments in the case; a periodic review section which includes all planning decisions and the reasons for them; and, especially for the child's future benefit, a "life story" book or equivalent such that is already used in good adoption practice (see Thomas and Beckford, 1999, pp. 80–89) but which we think should also be compiled whenever children are placed in long-term foster care.

---

[31] See report of the Department of Health (2000), '*Tracking Progress in Children's Services – an Evaluation of local responses to the Quality Protects Programme – Year 2*' at p. 66 in which reference is made to 'innovative integrated computer-based recording system being developed at Kensington and Chelsea'.

9 The need for a travelling record

When attempting to record social services involvement with the child and family prior to the most recent period of being looked after, we found that sometimes the information was missing because the child had moved from another authority. The implications of the non-transference of files are serious. These files hold all the previous case history as well as important medical, educational and personal information. It has been suggested that there should be a national travelling record, such as one would find in the NHS. Of course this is more difficult to achieve when authorities have differing systems of record-keeping, giving further weight to the argument for the need for nationally standardised local and compatible[32] record-keeping systems. Nevertheless, when a child or family move from one authority to another, the case file should always be transferred with them, contrary to existing practice. All that is necessary is that a clear reference of the file's current whereabouts remains with the exporting authority. It would be unthinkable for NHS medical records not to be transferred when a person moves to a different area. Why should social services files be any different?

10 Conclusion

This study is the third and most recent research of child placement, policy and practice which we have conducted for the Department of Health during the last 12 years (see Lowe *et al*, 1993; Murch *et al*, 1993; Lowe and Murch *et al*, 1999; Thomas and Beckford, 1999). In that time we have visited numerous social services departments, interviewed scores of social workers, as well as adoptive parents and some of their children. On the basis of this most recent study, we have reached a number of general conclusions about the current state and future prospects of the child placement services of England and Wales.

---

[32] See the discussion in Chapter 5 at pp. 124–126.

First, although it is inevitable in a policy-orientated research programme of this kind that problems in the system should be highlighted,
we should emphasise that we have come across many instances of skilled
and imaginative childcare practice – not least in this study where the
Government's Quality Protects Programme has stimulated a number of
important initiatives. As we observed in the *Supporting Adoption* study
(Lowe and Murch *et al*, 1999), our overriding impression remains that
the strength of the system lies in the dedication and commitment of many
staff to the children concerned, to their families and in the ways in which
the complex task of finding supportive stable placements are grappled
with. But, as we have commented upon before, structural weaknesses in
the system such as lengthy chains of command; inappropriate, mechanistic
and inflexible management; excessive pressure of work (often resulting
from competing responsibilities); inadequate childcare training for front-
line staff; and an over-emphasis on bureaucratic "paper pushing" all too
often mar the service.

In this particular study, perhaps the most serious problems we
encountered were in the two London authorities where we were disturbed
by the relatively high number of previous placements which children had
experienced (particularly in London High), and by the Directors' reports
of serious difficulties in staff recruitment and retention. We do not see
how a good quality childcare service which aims to bring stability to
children's lives can ever be achieved where, if the reports we received
were correct, there is such chronic staff instability and where up to half
the fieldworkers move on within six months.

Since this research was completed, a number of encouraging developments have taken place. The proposals in the White Paper on Adoption
have been translated into the Adoption and Children Bill, currently before
Parliament and equally importantly there are now key National Standards
on Adoption which are to be brought into force in 2003. We applaud
these developments, but they will need to be well resourced and backed
up by urgently needed measures which redefine more appropriately the
responsibilities of national and local government in this field. These
should aim at simplifying and reducing the chronic diversity in local
authority policy development and practice to which we have referred
above, and should ensure a much more consistent uniform level of

practice, for example, with respect to record-keeping. Also crucial to the success of the Government's plans will be the need to overcome the current shortage of adopters and long-term foster carers. We suspect this problem is dependent on the provision of necessary support services and a coherent nationwide system of financial allowances which are currently under review.

Somehow or other, it seems to us that circumstances have to be brought about in which childcare social work is rid of its prevailing state of low morale and where, as was the case in the decades immediately following the Second World War,[33] the child placement services attracted and retained committed high-quality and well-trained personnel who were enabled by the system to work closely with children and their families. Some of the Directors to whom we have spoken clearly know what should be aimed at and have demonstrated to us that they have the will to achieve it. It is now up to Government to extend its new thinking from adoption to all child placement services, especially to emphasise the positive role that long-term fostering can play and to back the creative elements in the field, whether or not, as we suspect, this will involve the restructuring of local authority social services.

We therefore welcome the announcement made by the Health Minister just as we were going to press[34] that there is to be a major review of fostering and placement choice which aims to provide stability for looked after children and a better framework of reward and support for foster carers.

References

Barth R (1999), 'Setting performance goals for adoption services: estimating the need for adoption of children in foster care', *Adoption Quarterly* Vol 2(3)

Department of Health (2000), *Tracking Progress in Children's Services: An evaluation of local responses to the Quality Protects Programme – Year 2*, London: Department of Health

---

[33] I.e. when there were specialist local authority children's departments.

[34] See the announcement made by Jacqui Smith on 20 March 2002 – Press Release: reference 2002/0145.

Harwin J and Owen M (2000), 'A study of care plans and their implementation and their relevance for Re W & B and Re W [care plan]', in Thorpe J and Cowton C (eds), *Delight and Dole: The Children Act 10 years on*, Jordans Publishing Ltd

Lowe N with Borkowski M, Copner R, Griew K and Murch M (1993), *Report of the Research into the Use and Practice of the Freeing for Adoption Provisions*, London: HMSO

Murch M, Lowe N, Borkowski M, Copner R and Griew K (1993), *Pathways to Adoption: Research project*, London: HMSO

Lowe N and Murch M, Borkowski M, Weaver A, Beckford V with Thomas C (1999), *Supporting Adoption – Reframing the approach*, London: BAAF

Rowe J, Cain H, Hundleby M and Keane A (1984), *Long-term Foster Care*, London: BAAF

Thomas C and Beckford V with Lowe N and Murch M (1999), *Adopted Children Speaking*, London: BAAF

Appendix

1 DATA COLLECTION FORMS

1.1 DCS1

Research Ref No: – .../.../....   SSDA 903 / Case No: ....

THE PLAN FOR THE CHILD: ADOPTION OR
LONG-TERM FOSTERING: DCS1

A: CHECK: (*See Essential Information Record Part 2 – Questions 46 & 48 for help with this*)

1) Child's date of birth (DD/MM/YY) (*no earlier than 1.4.86*)	
2) Gender	MALE / FEMALE
3) Looked after continuously during the year 1.4.98 – 31.3.99?	YES / NO
4) If **NO**, in & out three times or more during that year?	YES / NO
5) Date child last started to be looked after (DD/MM/YY)[1]	
6) **DOES THE CASE MEET THE ABOVE CRITERIA?**	YES (go on) / NO (stop)

B: LEGAL STATUS

	as at 31.3.99	as at 31.3.00
1) Legal Status (*See EIR2 Q46, P 6, ITEM 8 Code*)		
2) Reason being looked after (*See EIR2 Q46, P 7, ITEM 9 Code*)		

---

[1] *Not* the date of the last care episode.

C: PLAN FOR THE CHILD: *(See the last Care Plans before 31.3.99 & 31.3.2000, Q9.)*

Overall Plan	as at 31.3.99	as at 31.3.00
Enter Code number(s), see list on coding notes Additional coding space, if required		
If **Code 1**, enter time periods, if given on form or NoF		
If **Code 5**, enter time periods, if given on form or NoF		
If **Code 12** (Other), *specify*		
DATE PLAN AGREED *(See front of Care Plan or RoA Q6a)*		

D: STATUS OF THE CHILD as at 31.3.00:

Still being looked after as at 31.3.00? *(EIR2 Q46)*	YES / NO / NoF
If **NO**, *circle outcome* Placed for adoption & adopted / Formal discharge of care order / Return to birth family / Other	
If **Other**, *specify*	
IS THE CASE IN OR OUT OF THE CORE SAMPLE? If **OUT**, do DCS1 only. If **IN**, do DCS2 according to sampling criteria	IN / OUT
Current placement as at 31.3.00 *(See EIR2 Q48, P 9, DoH ITEM 10 code)*	

Other (not covered by DH, such as living with relatives/friends as relatives/friends	
If Other, *specify*	

Special Status Details: (*Tick as many as necessary*)

Freed for adoption	
Awaiting adoption order	
Awaiting adoption placement	
Awaiting long-term fostering placement	
Disrupted placement, plan the same	
Disrupted placement, plan being reassessed	
Other	
If **Other**, *specify*	
Has the plan for the child changed between 31.3.99 & 31.3.00?	YES / NO / NoF
If **YES**, give dates and reasons given for changes?	

E: DATA HELD & DATES OF EVENTS:

	Any copy on file?	Date of last on file
Care Plan	Y-LAC / Y-sso / NO	
Review of arrangements	YES / NO	
Essential information 1	YES / NO	
Essential information 2	YES / NO	

F: CHARACTERISTICS AT 31.3.99: (See EIR1, other forms may also be relevant)

Q2	Ethnic/racial origin of birth mother	
Q3	Ethnic/racial origin of birth father	
Q4	Child's cultural identity	
Q5	Does the child have a religion?	YES / NO / NoF Nominal / Practising / NoF
Q6	First language spoken	
Q7	Can child speak English fluently?	Fluently/ With difficulty / Not at all / Too young / NoF
Q10	Ongoing health conditions/disabilities	YES / NO / NoF
If **YES**, specify & add any other items (such as autism from BAAF Form E Q4);		

1.2   DCS2

Research Ref No: – ..../..../....   SSDA 903 / Case No: ....

THE PLAN FOR THE CHILD: ADOPTION OR
LONG-TERM FOSTERING: DCS2

File office location:

Names of key social worker(s): (The two most recent, see Care Plan Q23)

Name	Date noted in file

Names of Child Care Team Manager(s): (*The two most recent, see Care Plan Q23*)

Name	Date noted in file

G: CHARACTERISTICS AT 31.3.99: (*See EIR1, others may be required*)

EIR1 Q15	Mother's date of birth	
EIR1 Q16	Father's date of birth	
EIR1 Q17	Does the birth father have parental responsibility?	YES–Married / YES–Agreement / YES–Order / NO / NoF

H: OTHER SIGNIFICANT RELATIVES/ADULTS: (*See EIR1 Q18, Care Plan Q12, BAAF Form E Q4*)

Relative/ Adult	at 31.3.99		at 31.3.00		Other relevant information
Relationship to child	Type of contact (*See Codes*)	Frequency of contact (*Write in*)	Type of contact (*See Codes*)	Frequency of contact (*Write in*)	

I: SIBLINGS aged under 18 years old at 31.3.99: (i.e. born on or after 1.4.81) (*See EIR1 Q19 AND BAAF FORM E Q9*)

Follow the order the children have been placed in on the source document.

Gender M / F	Ethnic/ racial origin (*Write in*)	Date of birth	Who looks after the child? (*See Codes below*)	Relationship to child (*See Codes below*)	Placed or planned to be placed with this child	Note other relevant information (*such as reasons why siblings are not to be placed together*)
					YES / NO / NA / NoF	

Who looks after the Child Codes: 1 = Birth family, 2 = Other relatives (not as foster carers),
3 = Other relatives (as foster carers), 4 = local authority,
5 = Other *specify*, NoF = NoF

Relationship to Child Codes: 1 = Full, 2 = Step, 3 = Half, 4 = Adoptive

J: ESSENTIAL INFORMATION RECORD: Part 2

Dates of Reviews of Arrangements since the last Care Plan on file:

EIR2, Q38a	Individual education plan?	YES / Pending / NO / NoF
EIR2, Q38b & CP. Q12	Has the child been made the subject of a statement of special educational needs?	YES – still extant / YES – expired / NO assessment or statement / Pending / Statutory assessment only / NoF

K: PLACEMENTS: (See EIR2 Q48, Review of Arrangements Q1, BAAF Form E Q7)

Date placement began	Date placement ended	Type of placement (DH ITEM 10 Code)	Reason placement ended (Write in for post coding)	Was the move planned? YES / NO

		Birth mother	Birth Father
Evidence of any disruption(s) in a long-term placement?		YES / NO / NoF	
If **YES**, *specify when and what happened,*			
EIR2, Q50/52	Chronic conditions	YES / NO / NoF	YES / NO NoF
EIR2, Q51/53	Speak English fluently?	YES / NO / NoF	YES / NO NoF
	If NO, state first language		

L: **BAAF Form E:** (*See Q10*)

	Birth mother	Birth father
Marital status when child was born		
Marital status at 31.3.99		
Religion If **YES**, *specify*	Practising / Nominal / None / NoF	Practising / Nominal / None / NoF

M: CARE PLAN as at 31.3.99: (*See also BAAF Form E*)

CP Q3: Was the child and family known to the social YES / NO / NoF services department/voluntary agency prior to the date of placement?
If **YES**, give reasons for involvement and indicate what support was offered: CP Q6: What attempts have been made for the child to live with a relative or close family friend as an alternative to accommodation? (*Use None or NoF if applicable*)

Key source	Question	Birth mother	Birth father
CP Q12 & BAAFE1 Q10	Type of contact **at 31.3.99**		
	Frequency of contact **at 31.3.99**		
	Type of contact **at 31.3.00**		
	Frequency of contact **at 31.3.00**		

Care Plan/ RoA	Evidence of emotional or behavioural conditions requiring specialist services?	YES / NO / NoF
	If **YES**, are these specialist services in place?	YES / NO / NoF

Is there evidence of	Sexual abuse	YES / NoF	Emotional abuse	YES / NoF
	Physical abuse	YES / NoF	Neglect	YES / NoF

N: REHABILITATION

1) Was there ever a plan to rehabilitate? **If NO or NA, etc, go to section O**	YES / NO / NA (*as accommodated*) / NoF
2) If **YES**, to whom	
3) If **YES**, date when plan was made	
4) If **YES**, has the child ever been placed at home under supervision (home on trial)?	YES / NO / NoF
5) Date decision to end rehabilitation plan made	
6) Reasons given to end rehabilitation plan (*state if no reasons given or not on file*)	
7) Did the decision appear to have been postponed?	YES / NO / NoF
7a) If **YES**, give details (*state if no information available or not on file*)	

O: CHOICE OF ADOPTION OR LONG-TERM FOSTERING

See Review of arrangements, BAAF Form E Q11, Care Plan

1) Which option was chosen (*see DCS1*)	Adoption / Long-term foster care / Other
1a) If **Other**, *describe*	
2) Type of meeting where overall plan for the child first included a firm intention for adoption or long-term fostering	Care Plan / Review of arrangements / Fostering panel / Adoption panel

3) Date of this meeting	
4) Where was the child placed when the decision was made?	L -T Foster / S -T Foster / Residential / Friends or relatives / Other
4a) If **Other**, *specify*	

5) Were other alternative options considered (e.g. Living with other family members, residence order, adoption OR fostering) considered at this meeting? (*See RoA Q23m*)	YES / NO / NoF
5a) If **YES**, *specify what else was considered*	
5b) If **NO**, were reasons given for not considering any other options?	YES / NO / NoF
5c) If **YES**, *specify*	
6) Were reasons given for the option that was chosen?	YES / NO / NoF
6a) If **YES**, *specify*	

7) Persons 'consulted': (*See RoA Q17, 22, BAAF Form E Q11, Care Plan, Q8, 20, 21, 22*)

Name/Title	Invited	Present	Reports received	Decision *NOT* to consult?	Agreed?
Social worker					
Team manager					
Reviewing officer					
Child					
Birth mother					
Birth father					

7a) If a decision was made not to consult someone, *give details of why* (*Use NoF if applicable*)
7b) If anyone does not agree with the plan for adoption or fostering, *give details* (*Use NoF if applicable*)
8) Describe the evidence that the child's views were taken into account when this decision was made. (*See RoA Q17, BAAF Form E Q11, Care Plan Q20*) (*Use None or NoF if applicable*)

9) Did the decision appear to have been postponed?	YES / NO / NoF
9a) If **YES**, *Give details of reasons for postponement* (*e.g. change of social worker, cancelled meeting, referred back for further information from previous meetings*)	

R: SYNOPSIS:To be completed at any time.

(*To include brief care history, contact details, peculiarities of case, any unanswered questions which might be put to SW during interview*)

Any other comments about fostering or adoption:

Research Ref No: – .... ./.... ./....   SSDA 903 / Case No: ....

P: QUESTIONS ON PLAN FOR ADOPTION ONLY

1) Did/Are the birth parents contesting the adoption?	YES / NO / NoF
2) Was freeing for adoption considered?	YES / NO / NoF
2a) If **YES**, was a freeing order applied for?	YES / NO / NoF
2b) Date of freeing order (*if made, or write NA*)	
3) Have suitable adopters been identified for this child since the decision to plan for adoption was made?	YES / NO / NoF
3a) If **NO**, *give reasons why not* <u>(*Then go on to Q11*)</u>	

4) If **YES**, where were they found from? Other LA / Vol Agency / NoF	This LA /
5) Had this family fostered this child before they were identified as suitable adopters?	YES / NO / NoF
6) Date of adoption panel meeting when matching approved and placement for adoption with this family recommended	
7) Date of decision to place the child with this family	
8) Has the child now been placed for adoption with the family?	YES / NO / NoF
8a) If **NO**, *give reasons why not*	
9) Date of first court hearing for the adoption application (*or write NA if not at this stage*)	
10) Date of adoption order (*or write NA if not at this stage*)	
11) Describe any evidence of delay in finding a suitable adoption placement	

Research Ref No: – . . . ./. . . ./. . . .   SSDA 903 / Case No: . . . .

Q: QUESTION ON PLAN FOR LONG-TERM FOSTER CARE ONLY

1) Have suitable long-term foster carers been identified?	YES at the time of the decision / YES since the decision / NO / NoF
1a) If **NO**, *give reasons why not (Then go on to Question 8)*	
2) Date of decision by SSD to place child with these long-term foster carers	

3)	Has the child now been placed with these long-term carers? *(If **NO**, go to Any Other Comments)*	YES / NO / NoF
4)	Was the child living with this family at the time of the decision to place the child there?	YES / NO / NoF
5)	Date when the child first moved to this placement	
6)	Was this placement originally intended to be on a short- or long-term basis?	Long-term / Short-term / Undecided / NoF
7)	Has this family been approved as long-term foster carers? 7a) If **YES**, by whom? *(see BAAF FORM F)* 7b) If **NOT APPROVED**, *give details*	YES / NO / NoF Same LA / Other LA / Private agency / Other / NoF
8)	Is the child's current placement on a long-term basis?	YES / NO / NoF
	8a) If **YES**, *give details of why a change in placement necessary*	
9)	Describe any evidence of delay in finding a suitable long-term fostering placement (reasons may include, health, education, legal, contact, etc)	

2 INTERVIEW SCHEDULES

2.1 Social Workers Interview Schedule

SOCIAL WORKER QUESTIONNAIRE

Research code:

Name of key worker/team manager:

Location address:

Job title:

Local Authority:

Date of interview: Researcher:

A Social worker's experience:

A.1 How many years experience have you had dealing with childcare issues?

A.2 Roughly how many adoption cases have you dealt with in your social work career?

A.3 Do you feel your training has equipped you sufficiently when dealing with the long-term care of children?

Yes   No

(PROBE for details if necessary)

1 General questions about planning long-term care for "looked after" children

1.1 When you are making an assessment about the long-term care for a child, what factors do you bear in mind in relation to an **adoption or long-term fostering** placement? (post-code onto grid, transcribe if interesting or well expressed)

If absolutely necessary prompt from this list of factors

a) Relating to the child :

Factors	Adoption	Long-term fostering	Reasons and associated problems
Age			
Gender			
Ethnicity			
Culture			
Religion			
Language			
Physical disability			
Mental health illness			
Special educational needs			
Emotional/behavioural difficulties			
Child's views			
Length of time looked after			
Previous number/type of placements			
Child protection issue			
Future long-term needs of child			
Other (specify)			

b) Relating to the birth family:

Factors	Adoption	Long-term fostering	Reasons and associated problems
Part of sibling group Child's relationship with birth family (specify: mother, father, siblings, grandparents, other relatives)			
Type and frequency of contact with birth parents and/or siblings			
Wishes/views of birth parents/siblings/other family			
Availability and suitability of relatives/ friends as carers			
Mental health problems of either or both birth parents			
Drug/alcohol-related problems of either or both birth parents			
Other (specify)			

c) Relating to the carer

Factors	Adoption	Long-term fostering	Reasons and associated problems
Wishes/views of child's current carers			
Skills of child's current carers			
Other (specify)			

1.2a Turning to the local authority (hand card 4 to interviewee) which of these factors do you bear in mind in relation to an adoption or long-term fostering placement? (Tick as appropriate, state reasons briefly, try to grade factors in level of importance – only transcribe if interesting/well expressed)

Factors	Adoption	Long-term fostering	Reasons and associated problems
Team policy Review/Adoption panel policy (specify)			
Local authority policy/ guidelines you have to take into account on permanence, adoption or long-term fostering			
Availability of adopters/ long-term foster carers within your local authority area			
Presence within your local authority of voluntary adoption agencies or private foster carer agencies			
Membership of a regional consortium			
Availability of specialist services within your local authority for: a) mental health problems, either of birth parent(s) or child			
b) special educational needs			
c) physical disability			
d) Emotional/ behavioural difficulties			

Factors	Adoption	Long-term fostering	Reasons and associated problems
Allowance payments for: a) adoption b) fostering c) long-term fostering d) residence order			
Budgetary constraints within your department			
Effects of changes in local authority boundaries			
Views of your local authority legal department			
Views of local guardians *ad litem*			
Views of local Family Court judges			
Extent of support which can be offered to foster carers or adoptive families by the local authority			
Other (specify)			

1.2b Other factors not covered above (use this when post-coding if factors mentioned do not fit into other categories)

Factors	Adoption	Long-term fostering	Reasons and associated problems

1.3   The decision to place the child in a permanent long-term placement, whether adoption or long-term fostering, is governed by the needs of the child which are considered to be paramount. What do you understand by this?

1.4   What is your local authority's policy on rehabilitation?

    1.4.1   Are there specific guidelines which have to be followed in practice? (Specify)

    1.4.2   What factors may influence a decision to abandon rehabilitation in favour of long-term fostering or adoption?

1.5   Do you generally consider members of a child's extended family as potential carers or foster carers?

Carers	Foster carers
Yes / No	Yes / No
1.5.1 Why/why not?	Why/why not?

1.6   What is your local authority's policy on foster carers applying to adopt a child they are fostering?

1.7   What do you understand by each of the following terms and, what, if any, policy does your local authority have on each?

a) twin-tracking

LA policy:

b) contingency planning

LA policy:

c) concurrent planning

LA policy:

1.8   Do you have any views on:

a) the government's plans to increase the overall number of adoptions in the UK

b) a National Register of Adoption

2 Questions related to specific cases

Details about child in box to be completed before interview and used as a memory aide:

Research code: SSDA 903 Number:

Name of child (first name only   Age:
or removable post-it):
Gender: Male/Female

2.1   For how long have you been the key worker with this child?

INFORMATION WITHIN BOX TO BE COMPLETED BEFORE INTERVIEW AND CHECKED WITH SOCIAL WORKER

Child's special needs: Ethnicity
                        Culture
                        Religion
                        Language
                        Health
                        Education
                        Behaviour
                        Placement with siblings?

Long-term Care Plan for child: Adoption
                        Long-term fostering with 'stranger'
                        foster carers
                        Long-term fostering with relatives
                        Living with relatives/friends
                        Twin-tracking – specify both
                        Other (specify):

Date child first started to be looked after (ask only if not known):

No. of placements: Length of time of current placement:
(ask both, only if not known)

Up-to-date information about the case since DCS2 completed, with details:
(e.g. change of Care Plan, change/disruption of placement)

2.2   Were there any particular factors which influenced the choice of long-
      term Care Plan in this case?
      (Specify, with reasons and associated problems)

Factors	Adoption	Long-term fostering	Reasons and associated problems

3 Plan: Adoption (If plan long-term fostering, go to 4.)

3.1   When the decision was made, was long-term foster care considered as an
      alternative to adoption?

      Yes   No

      3.1.1 Why was it pursued/not pursued?

3.2   Were any other options considered as an alternative to adoption (e.g. living with relatives, family members as long-term foster carers, a residence order)?

Yes   No
Which and why?   Why not?

3.3   Did the original Care Plan have to be changed at any time?

Yes   No
In what way and why? (details)

3.4   Has a suitable adoptive family been identified since the decision to plan for adoption has been made?

Yes   No
What are the reasons why a suitable placement has not yet been found?

GO TO 5 (Questions arising out of case synopsis)

3.5   Was there any delay in making the decision to place the child for adoption with this family?

Yes   No
Give reasons.

GO TO 5 (Questions arising out of case synopsis)

4 Long-term fostering placement

4.1   When the decision was made, was adoption considered as an alternative to long-term fostering?

Yes   No

4.1.1 Why was it pursued/not pursued?

4.2   Were any other options considered as an alternative to long-term fostering? (e.g. living with relatives, family members as long-term foster carers, a residence order)?

Yes   No
Which and why?   Why not?

4.3   Did the original Care Plan have to be changed at any time?

Yes   No
In what way and why? (details)

4.4   Were suitable specific long-term foster carers identified at the time of the decision?

Yes   No

GO TO 4.4.3

4.4.1   Was the child living with this family at the time of the decision?

Yes / No

4.4.2   Was this placement **originally** intended to be on a short-term, adoptive or long-term basis?

Short-term   /   Adoptive   /   Long-term

Why did it change?

GO TO 5 (Questions arising out of case synopsis)

4.4.3   Is the child's current placement on a long-term fostering Basis?

Yes   No

Reasons for delay in finding a suitable long-term placement

5.   Specific questions arising out of case synopsis
     (to be prepared in advance)

THANK YOU FOR THE INTERVIEW

2.2   Directors' Interview schedule

SCHEDULE FOR DIRECTORS' INTERVIEWS

1   General views on adoption and long-term fostering policy

- Is there any written policy?
- How does it fit in with overall planning?
- The Director's personal involvement with policy-making.
- Who else is involved?
- How does he/she guarantee staff know the policy?
- Is it kept under review?
- How is it accessible to the public? (Accountability)
- If there is no written policy, how much is left to the discretion of the individual teams and how much autonomy do team managers have?

2   Staff development

- Experience, qualification and training of childcare staff.
- Staff recruitment and turnover.
- The Director's views on the specialism required for childcare work and placement including adoption and long-term fostering and working with families.
- Do they have a continuing professional development strategy, and if so how does it actually work?

3   Priority Issues

- Child protection.
- Rehabilitation.
- What role is there for adoption and long-term fostering?

- What support is there for adoption and long-term fostering? (Including adoption and fostering allowances.)
- What priority is given to working with families and direct work with children – is this left to foster carers?
- Budgetary constraints.

4 Record-keeping

- Why does it seem to be left to individual authorities to work it out rather than being done nationally?
- What access do children and parents have to records?

5 Drift

- What mechanisms are there for checking drift?
- Supervision of childcare plans.

6 How have they reacted to the Quality Protects initiative?

- What in the short term and the long term are both the benefits and the drawbacks of that initiative?

7 The dangers of league tables

8 The dangers of prioritising adoption

9 The viability issues concerning child placement services

- Is there a case for reorganisation of responsibilities? (Initially probe re: adoption and then long-term fostering)

10 Future initiatives

- In five years time what changes would you like to see in the delivery of childcare services, particularly for children who are clearly not going to return home?

11 A legal status for long-term fostering

12 Their views on a National Register of Adoption

3 Analysis of social work practitioner interviews

3.1 The sample

We interviewed a total of 26 social work practitioners, four in each local authority. As the pilot questionnaire was not substantially altered, the two pilot interviews, conducted in one of our participating authorities, have been included as part of the sample.

Of the 26 social work practitioners, 12 were team managers/leaders (this figure includes 1 service manager), 5 were senior social workers and 9 were basic grade social workers. Most of our interviews were conducted with social workers at a more senior level. We hoped to interview an equal number of basic grade and more senior social workers, particularly team managers, who we believed would have more of an overview of social work practice within their team and their authority, along with a wider knowledge of cases. Due to the need to complete the interview programme as quickly as possible, we were not always able to make contact with the basic grade social workers we wished to interview.

3.2 Years of experience in child care

Table A below shows how many years experience of child care each level of social worker had:

Table A
Number of years of child care experience of social work practitioner sample

No. of years experience	Team leaders/managers (including 1 service manager)	Senior social workers	Social workers
0–5 years	2	2	4
6–10 years	2		4
11–15 years	3		1
16–20 years	5	3	
TOTAL	12	5	9

As would be expected, the years of experience increase according to the level of the social worker.

3.3 Number of adoption cases dealt with

Note: There is no column in the table for the 21–50 adoption cases, as none of the respondents stated that they were part of this range.

Table B

Estimated number of years of childcare experience of social work practitioner sample

No. of years experience	No. of adoption cases							
	0	1–5	6–10	11–15	16–20	51–100	100+	TOTAL
0–5 years		4	2	2				8
6–10 years	1	2	1	1	1			6
11–15 years			2			1	1	4
15–20 years		2	1	1	2	2		8
TOTAL	1	8	6	4	4	3	1	26